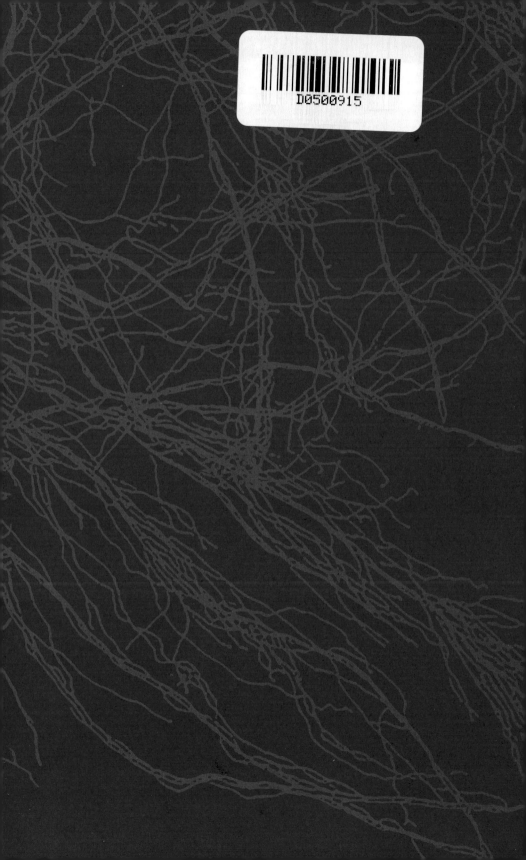

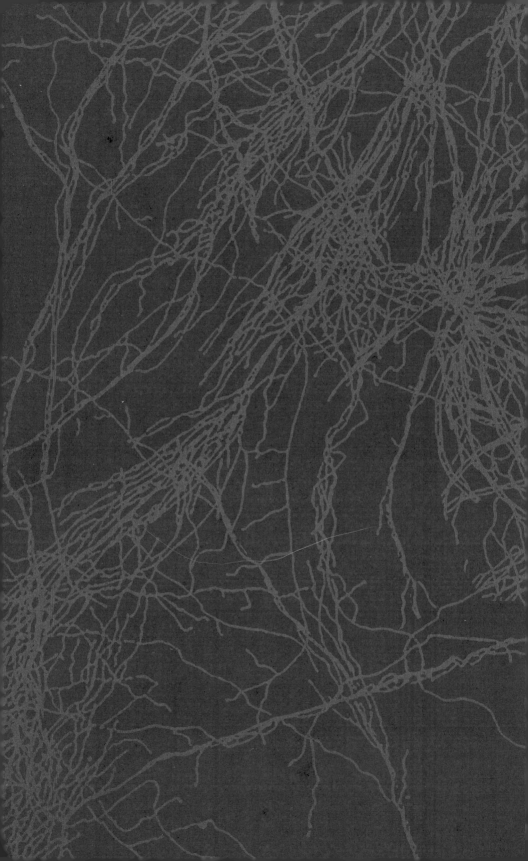

ADVANCE PRAISE FOR
THE ALGORITHMIC LEADER

"Provocative, powerful, and full of actionable wisdom. *The Algorithmic Leader* is a tour de force of ideas and insights from global pioneers who are challenging the status quo and reinventing organizations. Mike Walsh has produced a must-read for every leader and entrepreneur in this digital age."

Daniel Hulme, founder & CEO of Satalia

"This book first made me deeply uneasy, and then deeply inspired. Like you, I wrestle with how best to thrive as our world grows increasingly complex and confusing, a world where the simple rules just don't work anymore. Mike Walsh's 10 principles, distilled from real-life experience and deep thinking, point the way forward."

Michael Bungay Stanier, author of the *Wall Street Journal* bestseller *The Coaching Habit*

"Great companies are built on culture. Mike Walsh's prescient vision of the algorithmic company of the future is no robot army of soulless analytics dashboards, but a living, breathing organism—a community of humans who respond to motivation beyond compensation; purpose and impact; decision-making and autonomy; location and collaboration. A worthy read."

Brian Halligan, founder & CEO of HubSpot

"Mike Walsh provides an interesting and informative look at our future, which will be defined by algorithms and artificial intelligence. The underlying technologies may seem complex, but the message for business leaders is simple: use the new tools to enhance your skills—or become roadkill."

Vivek Wadhwa, distinguished fellow, Harvard Law School, Labor and Worklife Program and author of *The Driver in the Driverless Car*

"Mike Walsh's years of talking to the world's technology leaders have given him unusually deep insight into the ways in which technology will change our world. Now he has written a powerful book that enables the rest of us to gain that insight. This book will change the way you think. Full of rich examples and great quotes, it is like a hyperspeed trip into the future that will give you a whole new perspective on your industry and career."

Melissa Schilling, author of *Quirky* and *Strategic Management of Technological Innovation*

"Mike Walsh's *The Algorithmic Leader* is an intelligent and timely look at leadership in the digital age. If the twentieth century was governed by leaders of people, the twenty-first will be governed by leaders who understand the relationship between people and the technologies that define the modern workplace. Walsh exposes not just opportunities, but also potential pitfalls, ultimately leaving today's leaders smarter and better prepared for the coming rise of algorithms and big data."

Adam Alter, author of the *New York Times* bestseller *Irresistible* and *Drunk Tank Pink*

"I have read many thousands of pages about the impact of algorithms and automation on our lives, and Mike Walsh's *The Algorithmic Leader* stands out from the crowd. It is honest in its complexity, practical in its lessons, and profound in its analysis of the future of work. It's a must-read for anyone contemplating how smart humans can collaborate with smart machines."

David Epstein, author of the *New York Times* bestseller *The Sports Gene* and *Range*

"*The Algorithmic Leader* is brilliant and scary. The scale of change that AI is bringing into our lives can be bewildering. In this timely book, Mike Walsh provides (often counterintuitive) ideas and fascinating insights into what the coming decades will bring. Read it twice, or to be safe, three times. This is an essential book."

Efe Cakarel, founder & CEO of MUBI

"We are at the dawn of the artificial intelligence era. Mike Walsh offers a succinct guide for leaders to understand the secrets of the new algorithmic age, and how they apply in a disruptive and diverse global context. You cannot grasp the future of AI without considering Asia. Understanding leaders like Jack Ma and Masayoshi Son is as important as learning from Jeff Bezos or Reed Hastings. Whether you are working in San Francisco or Shanghai, *The Algorithmic Leader* is a cognitive tool kit for changing the way we think, how we work, and what it takes to win in an increasingly uncertain future."

Porter Erisman, former Alibaba vice president and author of *Alibaba's World*

"Mike Walsh has always been a fine teller of the future's stories. But this book is different. It offers not just a way of thinking about the future, but also a set of pragmatic and practical frameworks for navigating them. Oh yeah, and the stories are great too."

Genevieve Bell, director of the 3A Institute, Florence Violet McKenzie Chair, distinguished professor at the Australian National University, vice president and senior fellow at Intel Corporation

"If you want to start asking the right questions about the future, then Mike Walsh's new book is the best place to start. In an age of artificial intelligence, we all need to reconsider ideas around privacy, privilege, power, equality, and even truth. *The Algorithmic Leader* provides strategies, frameworks, and importantly, provocations designed to wake us up to the fact that our world may look the same, but all the rules have changed."

Sean Gourley, founder & CEO of Primer

"Mike Walsh is challenging the old models of management. He paints a future for leadership that has a lot more in common with the art of gardening than the art of war. Great gardeners start with a great vision and then focus on creating an ecosystem that understands, nourishes, and tends, allowing all to become their strongest, no matter what uncertainties they face, until they brilliantly fruit and blossom. Walsh's principles tell us how it should be done, but then he passionately shows that it is not the 'how' that matters but the 'why': to make our world a better place for all of humanity to flourish."

Ali Parsa, founder & CEO of Babylon Health

THE

ALGORITHMIC

LEADER

How to be smart when machines are smarter than you

Mike Walsh

THE
ALGORITHMIC
LEADER

TOMORROW

Cataloguing in publication information
is available from Library and Archives Canada.
ISBN 978-1-989025-33-8 (hardcover)
ISBN 978-1-989025-34-5 (ebook)

Page Two Books
www.pagetwobooks.com

Design by Peter Cocking
Editing by Amanda Lewis
Printed and bound in Canada by Friesens
Distributed in Canada by Raincoast Books
Distributed in the US and internationally
by Publishers Group West, a division of Ingram

19 20 21 22 23 5 4 3 2

www.mike-walsh.com

*"Se vogliamo che tutto rimanga come è,
bisogna che tutto cambi."*

"For things to remain the same, everything must change."

GIUSEPPE TOMASI DI LAMPEDUSA,
IL GATTOPARDO

In memory of Brian Walsh, my father and
the greatest leader I've ever known

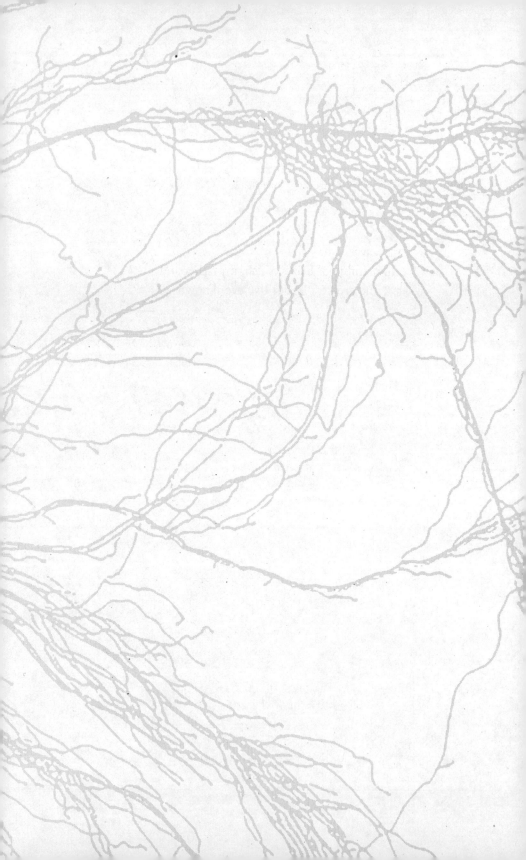

CONTENTS

INTRODUCTION
WELCOME TO
THE ALGORITHMIC AGE

"A rhizome has no beginning or end; it is always in the middle, between things, interbeing, intermezzo."
GILLES DELEUZE AND FÉLIX GUATTARI

Flying the unfriendly skies

The scene at the boarding gate was nothing out of the ordinary. Anxious parents with young children milled around the front of the lineup, arms overflowing with bags and toys. Behind them, a cluster of first-class travelers tapped impatiently at their phones, while those holding boarding cards with zones 5 or below eyed their carry-on luggage, wondering if they would be forced to check their bags.

Certainly, few of the passengers scheduled to fly on that cloudy, late Sunday afternoon in April would have paid any heed to the automated systems that were already in action as they filtered through security, boarding passes in hand, and made their way to United flight 3411, due to depart Chicago for Louisville at 5:40 p.m.

1

At around thirty minutes before the scheduled departure time, over the rhythmic beeping of passengers scanning their barcodes, a gate agent announced that the flight had been overbooked and that volunteers were required to give up their seats for United employees who needed to get to Louisville. The agent offered a $400 voucher and an overnight hotel stay in Chicago. Given that the next available flight was not for twenty-one hours, it was not surprising that no one took up the offer.

By now, most of the passengers were on board. With no volunteers, the same request was made over the plane's intercom, this time with a voucher for $800. When no one responded once again, a tense United manager boarded and declared to the passengers that some of them would now be chosen at random to leave the plane.

Of course, there was nothing actually *random* about the process. Passengers were chosen by the airline's computer system, based on a complex set of data and calculations. Four passengers were selected, three of whom grudgingly complied, taking their belongings off the plane. The fourth refused.

At 5:21 p.m., another passenger, Tyler Bridges, posted on Twitter a video that subsequently went viral. The contents were shocking and inexplicable: a passenger with blood running down his face could be seen running up the center aisle of the plane, shouting, "I have to go home! I have to go home!" and then, "Just kill me. Just kill me."

More videos emerged on social media shortly after. In one, police officers appeared to be escorting passengers from the plane. In another, a man was dragged violently out of his seat, onto the floor, and then off the plane by a Chicago Department of Aviation officer, as other passengers screamed in protest. It later emerged that the removed passenger was the fourth passenger, the one who had refused to give up his seat. His name was David Dao, and he lived in Louisville, Kentucky.

Sixty-nine-year-old Dao, a US citizen, was originally from Vietnam. He went to medical school there in the 1970s before moving to the United States after the fall of Saigon. A pulmonary disease specialist, he wanted to stay on the flight because he had patients to see the following morning.

Despite his protests, Dao had been forcibly removed by an airport security team so violently that he suffered a slew of injuries, including a concussion, a broken nose, and the loss of two front teeth. After his removal, a United crew took the newly vacated seats and finally, almost two hours after the scheduled departure time, flight 3411 took off. That was, however, only the beginning of the story.

Later that evening, online interest in the event grew as more people watched and shared the violent scenes of Dao's removal. United Airlines was forced to issue a statement to the media to explain what had happened:

> Flight 3411 from Chicago to Louisville was overbooked. After our team looked for volunteers, one customer refused to leave the aircraft voluntarily, and law enforcement was asked to come to the gate. We apologize for the overbook situation. Further details on the removed customer should be directed to authorities.

Overbooking is one of those evils of modern-day flying that travelers have come to accept. Airlines assume that there will be a certain number of no-shows on any given day. Accordingly, they oversell tickets, knowing that even if everyone turns up, some people with more flexible schedules can be persuaded to accept compensation in return for catching an alternative flight. In this situation, however, no one wanted to give up their seat. And with a flight crew that needed to board, that meant that ticketed and seated passengers had to be removed.

You might think that such a decision was merely the result of poor customer service. United, after all, already had something of a poor reputation when it came to looking after passengers. Numerous jokes circulated online about the airline breaking guitars, losing luggage, and even killing pets.

But what if flight 3411's problems were not the fault of a gate agent or flight attendant, but rather a very different kind of failure? United was a company driven by rules, with strict operating procedures. And importantly, the execution of those rules and procedures was largely governed by data and algorithms. Few employees at United had the power to deviate from the airline's algorithmic playbook; employees were under pressure to follow, not bend, the rules.

A cascade of algorithms shaped the events of that fateful day. An employee-scheduling algorithm optimized for efficiency determined that crew should be loaded thirty minutes before a flight, even though passengers had already boarded. A yield-management algorithm optimized for profit, which generally controlled the overbooking ratio, had set the maximum compensation allowable for bounced travelers at $800. Finally, a customer-value algorithm, optimized to avoid annoying the highest-spending flyers, was designed to identify budget travelers, who were the least likely to cause problems should they need to be "re-accommodated."

"Re-accommodation," in case you were wondering, is the term that United's CEO, Oscar Munoz, initially used to describe Dao's violent removal from the plane. "This is an upsetting event to all of us here at United," Munoz was quoted as saying. "I apologize for having to re-accommodate these customers."

Munoz had been in the job for about a year and a half before that Sunday's crisis. Charismatic, funny, and well loved by his employees, he had come from humble beginnings: he grew up in Southern California, where his father had been a union meatcutter from Mexico. After working his way up the ranks of companies like PepsiCo and Coca-Cola, he had his real leadership breakthrough as COO of rail operator CSX, where he had artfully steered the railway toward more profitable product segments and tighter operating efficiency, ultimately resulting in its market capitalization quadrupling over the twelve years he spent in leadership positions there.

When Munoz was offered the job as CEO of United, the airline was in trouble. Not only was the company reeling from a bribery scandal involving public officials, but it was also suffering integration woes as a result of its 2010 merger with Continental. In 2015, United tied with Southwest for the lowest on-time arrival rate. Morale was low, employees were disengaged, and the two hedge funds that were the airline's largest shareholders were demanding changes.

Munoz had seen the dangers of a disengaged workforce and lack of operational discipline firsthand at CSX. He immediately set to work rebuilding trust with employees and implementing tighter controls. A week after accepting the job as CEO, he emailed the company's most frequent flyers, promising, "We can do better." The early response from analysts, the industry, and even the unions was positive.

Then, thirty days later, Munoz had a massive heart attack that nearly killed him. However, he had a heart transplant, which saved his life. His recovering health seemed to take on a life of its own at United, becoming a metaphor for the hopeful rebirth of the company. He had become one of the most respected corporate leaders in the US, and things were looking up for United.

Then David Dao decided to not give up his seat.

It is understandable that Munoz's first response was to defend his team. They had, after all, followed the company playbook to the letter. Shortly after the incident, he sent employees a memo supporting their decisions, while characterizing Dao as "disruptive and belligerent." Only in the face of global outrage would he rapidly shift his position.

And outrage there was. In just under a month, Munoz fell dramatically from grace. He would be forced to issue a series of progressively more humble apologies, provide testimony to Congress, reach an out-of-court settlement with Dao, and forgo his planned appointment as chairman of the airline. Suddenly, his recent designation as *PR Week*'s Communicator of the Year, awarded to him just a few months earlier, became an ironic reminder of how quickly circumstances could change.

Where did Munoz go wrong? In almost every respect he was the model corporate leader: principled, fair, and admired by his employees. Even his focus on operational discipline at the expense of customer service was not an unreasonable trade-off in an industry driven by small margins and high competition. To understand why Munoz's approach was flawed, you have to look at the problem again, but with a different lens.

Munoz was an ideal leader for an era of maintenance schedules, quarterly budgets, cost reductions, sales quotas, and margin improvements. While those things are certainly important, they are no longer sufficient for survival. They are part of an analogue world of people, assets, and things.

Events used to happen at a relatively more measured and predictable pace. You could invest in products and platforms, and amortize the development costs over long life cycles. Planning departments created detailed budgets, which allowed managers to scrutinize sales performance quarter to quarter, month to month, week to week, item by item.

That's not to say that the job of the leader was more straightforward then. If anything, mature industries exhibit a fierce struggle for market share. This Darwinian environment selects for a particular kind of leader—aggressive, ruthless, with a win-at-all-costs mentality—but the skills formed and valued in one era will not necessarily serve you well in a new one characterized by different rules and dynamics. Munoz ran into trouble when he didn't recognize that the real driver of success or failure for an airline like United, and many other companies, is not its stuff but rather its algorithms.

United didn't have a customer service problem; it had an algorithmic design problem.

You don't have to be working for a technology company for algorithms to matter. Every company today is an algorithmic company, whether it knows it or not. What is a car these days but a software platform on wheels? When the leaders of Volkswagen failed to stop their own engineers from designing software to allow their diesel cars to pass US emissions tests, regulators branded the entire company a criminal enterprise.

There is no escaping algorithms. Information about the world reaches us through data; our decisions and attempts to change the world are expressed in data. Algorithms are not purely abstractions. They are a bridge between computation and real-world challenges. We use them as a tool to address problems in an increasingly complex world.

Algorithms shape the design and delivery of products and services, with profound implications not only for how we work but also for how we solve problems and manage people. They present powerful opportunities for those who know how to work with them. In a way, algorithms are a form of embodied logic, in cases where they are well defined. They allow us to take our knowledge, experience, and insights about the world and build them into platforms that can then act autonomously on our behalf. Some are deterministic, while others may have a random component that increases their efficiency in computing problems.

The drama on flight 3411 could have happened on almost any airline, all of which have similar algorithmic models, or in any number of other industries—from banking to retail, logistics to insurance. And in fact, you will find that algorithms are increasingly at the heart of major scandals and strategic challenges in a wide range of companies. Poor management of customer information and algorithmic security at Experian, Equifax, and Target led to massive data breaches. Facebook's Mark Zuckerberg faced days of heated interrogation on Capitol Hill for the company's repeated misuse of consumer data and their irresponsible attitude toward allowing third parties to manipulate their algorithms. And in February 2018, Uber settled (to the tune of $245 million) with a Google subsidiary, Waymo, when an engineer Uber hired brought over proprietary algorithms, data, and research used for the production of self-driving cars.

Algorithms are here to stay. The secret lies in knowing how to lead companies and organizations that use and depend on them; that's where Munoz fell down. But just how did algorithms become so important to our collective future? And how can someone trained in the analogue era truly rise to become an algorithmic leader?

A tale of two leaders

Just as there is no single path to success, there is also no definitive archetype for what makes for a great algorithmic leader. The aim of this book is to explore the personal qualities, cognitive frameworks, and strategic approaches exhibited by a small but growing group of leaders who seem to thrive in this new environment, which is really about finding your own response to the algorithmic age. As a starting point, I've created this simple definition:

> An algorithmic leader is someone who has successfully adapted their decision making, management style, and creative output to the complexities of the machine age.

To be a successful leader in this new era requires a different approach, a different set of skills, and a different way of thinking. But by now, perhaps a more existential question may be troubling some of you: *Isn't the very idea of a leader in the algorithmic age an antiquated concept?*

If in the future companies are composed of not only people but also algorithmic platforms that are making decisions, monitoring processes, and managing resources, what exactly will be the role of the leader? Can you be a leader if you aren't making all the important decisions? Can you be a leader without an impressive job title and a team of subordinates? Can you even be a leader without people following you?

We like to tell ourselves stories about leaders. Whether it be classical myths or Hollywood movies, business biographies or news stories, we tend to present leaders as individuals with special qualities who act as heroic agents of change, defending their people against enemies and bringing them safely into a promised land of prosperity.

The problem is, in an algorithmic world, the traditional distinctions—that is, those between competitor and partner, local and global, boss and subordinate, center and edge, customer and product, human and machine—are all blurred. Data and algorithms now connect us in complex, dynamic ways that make a mockery of the neatly arranged models of twentieth-century organizations, industries, and societies.

If the analogue leader thrived by climbing the heights of a hierarchical organization, the algorithmic leader needs to operate in an interconnected totality that is more like an organic ecosystem.

Those of you who are entrepreneurs or freelancers have an advantage: You already understand that being in a small organization means playing multiple roles. You have already mastered the art of orchestrating other suppliers and technologies in order to bring a complex product or service to market, despite your size. When you are small, your value as a leader is defined not by your position in an organizational chart or a title on your business card, but by the map of your connections and relationships.

Leaders in large organizations need to learn this same lesson about how real value is created. Knowledge in a twenty-first-century organization lives everywhere, not just where the corporate phone directory says it belongs. Insight is democratic. The next great idea that will transform your business might be hidden in your server logs, in field notes written by a maintenance engineer, or buried in your product itself, like the live data from a jet engine operating at 35,000 feet.

Your real power as a leader is reflected not in how many people you have reporting to you, but in how successful you have been in connecting people, partners, and platforms. You add the most value when you grow and feed your organizational network, not when you push your way to the top of the corporate pyramid.

The leader in the rhizome

In the 1970s, two French philosophers, Gilles Deleuze and Félix Guattari, challenged existing philosophical notions of the construct of knowledge, arguing that the traditional Western comparison of knowledge to a tree restricted it to being a series of vertical and linear connections. They noted that the tree model (which they call the arborescent model) had come to dominate Western thought in a plethora of disciplines and areas of study, whether it be linguistics, psychoanalysis, logic, biology, or human organization. In essence, the tree model means we approach knowledge as a hierarchical system, with knowledge growing from roots, just as a tree does.

Deleuze and Guattari found that model of describing the world inadequate to explain the multiplicity of human society and culture. In their view, there was a more appropriate metaphor from the natural world: the rhizome.

A rhizome is the tangled mass of roots of plants like bamboo, lotus, or ginger. Rhizomes are stems that run underground, striking new roots out of their nodes, down into the soil. They can also shoot new stems up to the surface. The rhizome is a complex network used not only for reproduction, but also for storing nutrients and energy for all new plants that are propagated from it. If you have ever tried to rid your garden of an invasive species like poison ivy or nettle, you have experienced the irrepressible power of a rhizome. Even a small piece left in the soil after you have dug out a weed will be enough for a new plant to emerge.

Whereas a tree has only one trunk and one entry point, a rhizome has lateral shoots and probing roots, and hence multiple entryways. A rhizome has ceaseless connections; there is no beginning or end. And in this way, Deleuze and Guattari argue that the rhizome helps us see that history and culture create a complex map with a wide array of influences of no specific origin or genesis.

The rhizome is also a useful way of thinking about leadership in an algorithmic age.

If the analogue leader was a rigid tree—supported by a root system of administrative processes, with subordinates as branches stemming from them—then the algorithmic leader is something very different indeed. Like a rhizome, algorithmic leaders have to thrive without clearly defined hierarchies or structures. You need to be a connector, not a controller. You are an integral part of a root system that has no center or edge and that relies on you to feed it nutrients and expand its connections. Just as no single shoot of bamboo is in charge of the forest, neither are you solely responsible for the fate of your team or organization. But that doesn't mean you can't be influential, powerful, or even as pervasive and resilient as a weed.

The rhizome is a reminder that in an age where machine intelligence is able to continuously weave meaningful connections between data, we must challenge all of our traditional notions about structure, hierarchy, and order.

Being an algorithmic leader means more than just being able to share a few rehearsed anecdotes about artificial intelligence and big data. It means learning to tamp down your own ego, willingly tearing down the corporate structures that support your status, letting go of the idea that you need to make all the decisions, letting your teams self-organize and self-manage, not worrying about being seen to be right all the time, being open to more open forms of partnerships and work arrangements, and embracing a new, uncertain future.

As I've watched the rise of Netflix in recent years, and the way it has transformed global TV-watching habits, I have often wondered how an old-school media mogul like Rupert Murdoch, John Malone, or Ted Turner might have run that business. What made the CEO of Netflix, Reed Hastings, so effective? How was he able to achieve such rapid global growth at Netflix while navigating difficult transitions, such as when the company switched from sending physical DVDs in the mail to embracing broadband streaming? Is Netflix successful because it runs on algorithms, or because it is run by algorithmic leaders?

I had an interesting insight into that question when I met Andy Harries, the CEO and co-founder of Left Bank Pictures. Harries is one of the world's top drama creators, including *Cold Feet*, *Prime Suspect*, *Wallander*, *Outlander*, and *The Queen*, which saw Helen Mirren win, among other awards, an Oscar for Best Performance by an Actress in a Leading Role.

Harries wanted to pitch a TV show about the British royal family, based on themes explored in *The Queen*. He met with all the major US TV networks, who liked the idea but, after lots of consideration and debate, couldn't commit to moving forward. Finally, Harries decided to meet with Reed Hastings and Netflix's chief content officer, Ted Sarandos.

It was the strangest meeting, Harries explained, as he handed me a cup of a coffee at his office in London. As soon as he walked into the conference room with Hastings and Sarandos, and before he had a chance to pitch the show, they told him that they were ready to move ahead. And not just with a pilot, but with a full season.

Unlike the other networks, the team at Netflix had already analyzed their audience data and had used algorithms to predict the show's likely performance. They knew their audience and precisely the kinds of shows that would work. Furthermore, with an upcoming launch in the UK market, they believed that the proposed show would be a hit. And they were right. *The Crown*'s third season is now in production, and it has twice been nominated for an Emmy for Outstanding Drama Series.

Algorithmic leaders reveal themselves in the way they make decisions and solve problems. How Reed Hastings and his team think about content, its relationship to their audience and their platform, and even how it should be presented and released is radically different from the way traditional leaders in media companies act and behave.

When you are capable of knowing precisely what any of your millions of global customers are doing or desiring at any point in time, how can you not see the world differently? How can you not seek to leverage machine learning, algorithms, and automation to fulfill those needs in a highly personalized way?

Leaders like Hastings didn't always have that kind of perspective. Most of us who are currently in leadership positions started out as analogue leaders. We need to make a conscious decision to adapt and evolve and to recognize that the availability of data and algorithms should change our viewpoint.

The end of all jobs?

This book is about how algorithms, AI, and automation will change the world of work, including your job as a leader. There are some, however, who take a much darker view and believe that the machine age will radically eliminate work itself. Let's address that now.

When I finished high school, I chose to pursue two degrees: accounting and law. But after spending a couple of months during my summer vacation stuck in a basement combing through records for an insurance audit, I knew that accounting was not for me. That left the legal profession.

Law firms are conservative places: heavy furniture, wood paneling, portraits of the founding partners, and lots of leather-bound books. On my first day as a graduate, I pulled on my brand new suit, which was deeply uncomfortable and fit terribly, and tried to put on a brave face as I joined the other new recruits waiting in the conference room. When it came time to meet the managing partner, he fixed me with a grim look. He had a tall stack of legal briefs in front of him: curling papers, bulldog clips, and beige manila folders.

"Ah, the new associate..." He smiled, with the charm of an apex predator. "Do you see all these documents?" He gestured at the pile. "We need you to check them all for spelling by the morning."

"Spelling?" I croaked, looking at the pile with horror, wondering why I had spent five years in law school.

"Yes," he replied, "the lawyers around here are useless. Their briefs are full of errors. Your job is to find them."

"Don't you have any software for that?" I asked, the prospect of years of menial labor now stretching ahead of me.

"Yes, actually, we do." He sighed, dismissing me with his hand. "That's you."

Suffice to say, I didn't last long. When I quit the internship and the legal profession as a whole, I found myself thinking, "If these lawyers can't even use basic technology, what hope is there for them?" Probably, I surmised, most of them would end up being replaced by software. After all, it seemed that a lot of legal work could be done by using better templates, expert systems, and document analysis software.

I cringe now to think of my naivety. That was over twenty years ago. Not only has technology not replaced the legal profession, but there are more lawyers now than at any time in history (a terrifying thought!). How could I have got it so wrong?

I believe that the mistake I made then is one that many are making now. People who argue that robots will take away all our jobs assume that there is a simple relationship between automation and employment. They believe that just because you can automate part of a job, the entire job will be automated at some point. But sometimes technology has the effect of *changing* jobs rather than cutting them. As we will examine later in this book, the ATM didn't mean the end of the bank teller. The number of bank tellers eventually increased, as it became cheaper to open up bank branches. The real impact of automation was to change the job of the bank teller from counting money to building relationships.

Back to our legal friends. A little while ago, eDiscovery software started to catch on. This software does a lot that a junior legal associate might do in a court case: reading through documents, compiling lists, organizing materials. It is much less expensive to use eDiscovery than a human to do that work, which means that judges started allowing it more often, which then generated more work for lawyers. In other words, automating part of a lawyer's job led to greater access to legal services and a corresponding increase in demand for lawyers.

But while algorithms might not necessarily replace the need for human beings, they do increase the responsibility placed on us. Think back to the experience of Oscar Munoz and his disastrous response to what happened on flight 3411: An algorithm cannot be a stand-in for true leadership. We still need real-life humans who can interpret what the machines are telling us, who can decide whether those conclusions are appropriate and ethical, and who know how to best orchestrate the capabilities of machines that are smarter than us.

Unlike a human being, an algorithm will come to the same conclusions every single time, whether it is Monday morning or Friday afternoon, cold or hot, or after the algorithm has handled thousands of similar cases. However, that doesn't make algorithms impartial judges. Quite the contrary.

Algorithms are trained on data that is collected by and about humans. We choose where the data comes from, what success criteria are used, or what truth looks like, and in doing so, we embed them with all our views, prejudices, and biases. They are ultimately an expression of us and our world. While we may end up making fewer decisions in the future, leaders will need to spend more time designing, refining, and validating the algorithms that will make those decisions instead.

Anyone can be an algorithmic leader, even people who don't work in what we might think of as a large, algorithmic organization like Amazon, Google, or Facebook. That is because big or small, traditional or technological, algorithms and data are changing every kind of business.

Whether you run a big factory making automotive parts in China or a small dry cleaner in Brooklyn, your success hangs on more than how well you manage your staff, customers, or suppliers. In fact, your future is more likely to depend on how well you leverage all the data and information generated by your activities rather than how well you manage the typical levers of your business.

Let's consider those two cases: one big, one small. If you are an automotive manufacturer, your physical factory has a digital footprint. The performance of your machines, the configuration of your production lines, the design of your workflows and processes can all be expressed as data that can be read, managed, and optimized by algorithms. It can even be copied and transplanted as a template to somewhere else entirely. That means a digital facility designed in Shenzhen, China, can be replicated in Warsaw, Poland. In other words, the most important part of your factory is the data about your factory.

Similarly, even if you run a small dry cleaning business, your engagement with customers, your accounting systems, your energy and chemical consumption, your scheduling of part-time staff all generate a digital footprint, which in the near future might be optimized, for a monthly subscription cost, by cloud-based software that uses machine learning and AI. You will still work in a physical store, but many of your decisions, customer interactions, and daily activities will be driven by code.

The future of companies, regardless of size, will be shaped by algorithms. It is already happening today. Think about it. What processes based on algorithms are currently in place in your organization? (Are your customers, partners, or employees even aware of the automated systems that shape their lives, decisions, and experiences?)

Not every business will have the resources to create its own machine learning team, design its own algorithms, or disrupt its entire industry. However, none of those things are necessary in order for you to become a more effective leader, capable of weathering the uncertainties of the twenty-first century. As a starting point, it is helpful to realize that you are not actually fighting the machines for survival. Not yet, anyway.

We have a bad habit of fighting the future. Whether it be John Henry in a race with a steam-powered rock-drilling machine, chess champion Garry Kasparov against IBM's Big Blue, or Lee Sedol, the world's best Go player, against Google's AlphaGo AI, we love the idea of pitting ourselves against our own innovations. But when a human loses against a machine, is not the real winner the humans who built the machine? For leaders, the real question is not how smart machines can be, but rather *What does "smart" now mean when it comes to humans?*

Surviving the algorithmic age doesn't require you to *be smarter than* machines. You just need to know what it takes to *be smart*.

Being smart is about knowing the right way to do things; avoiding unnecessary steps; not wasting time or resources; and being open to new approaches and fresh ideas. It is not about blindly following trends. It is about knowing how to take advantage of the latest thinking and applying it effectively to practical problems. Being smart today is different than it was fifty—or even five—years ago.

Being smart when machines are smarter than you requires you to become something new.

How to read this book

This book is based on 10 principles that I've organized into three stages of a journey of transformation, starting with your own mindset, then extending to the people with whom you work, and finally expanding to the world around you:

I   Change Your Mind
II Change Your Work
III Change the World

A word of warning. The principles in this book are neither exhaustive nor definitive; they are intended as a guide for personal exploration. I chose them based on numerous conversations with visionary leaders and global innovators, a decade of advisory and consulting work, and a detailed study of scenarios where algorithmic-era leaders typically act and think differently from analogue-era leaders. So, while you can certainly read the table of contents as a series of recommendations, what I'm really trying to offer you is not a checklist but a practical framework for thinking about problems and decisions in a new way.

The 10 principles are:

1   Work backward from the future
2   Aim for 10×, not 10%
3   Think computationally
4   Embrace uncertainty
5   Make culture your operating system
6   Don't work, design work
7   Automate and elevate
8   If the answer is X, ask Y
9   When in doubt, ask a human
10 Solve for purpose, not just profit

Read this book from start to finish, or skip around and focus on the principles that interest you most. In the real world, ideas have to speak to difficult choices that leaders face when they make decisions, allocate resources, or bet on a new venture. So, as you read, try to apply the principles to your current challenges and opportunities.

At the end of each chapter, I've included a short summary and a question designed to challenge you to confront the core of what needs to change in your own organization. It is all too easy to read about disruption without accepting the terrifying possibility that the real thing that needs to change isn't your company or industry—it's you.

PART I

CHANGE YOUR MIND

WORK BACKWARD FROM THE FUTURE

*"I believe myself to possess a most singular combination of
qualities exactly fitted to make me preeminently a discoverer
of the hidden realities of nature."*

ADA LOVELACE

Start with algorithms

Imagine what life might be like in ten years.

Perhaps you are picturing fleets of self-driving cars on the road, drones delivering packages, fully automated factories, and thinner, sleeker, and faster devices. These are all realistic possibilities, given current circumstances and developments, and yet, hardly a dramatic departure from the appearance of daily life today. But while our technological hardware may not radically change in the next decade, there is one thing that does stand to radically change: our experiences.

All of our experiences of how we do things—communicate, shop, find love or work, get paid, travel—are likely to change as a result of algorithms. In the future, as we are better able to leverage data with machine learning and computation, we will see exponential improvement in the algorithmic platforms that shape our world. And the associated new algorithmic experiences, rather than operational improvements as a result of algorithms, are likely to be where the greatest business value is created.

First, let's clear up a common misconception: algorithms are not some computational incantation that somehow bring machines to life. They are more like a recipe for baking a cake: a step-by-step process (mixing ingredients) to solve a problem (you need a cake for your son's birthday party).

The very concept of an algorithm predates the modern computer by several thousand years; it can be traced back to some of the greatest minds of the ancient world who also used algorithms to think through difficult challenges.

For example, imagine you have a pleasant, shady rectangular courtyard behind your house, which you plan to cover with square stone tiles. Your stonemason asks you what size tile to order, and now you have a bit of a dilemma. What is the largest size you can pick that will allow you to evenly tile the entire 38- × 16-foot surface?

Greek mathematician Euclid had a method for solving this dilemma. Tiling your courtyard is a mathematical puzzle that can be solved by computing the greatest common divisor (GCD) of two numbers—that is, the largest number that divides both of them without leaving a remainder. Euclid's procedure for performing the calculation, which he first described in his book *Elements* (c. 300 BC), is one of the oldest algorithms that we still use.

The Euclidean Algorithm, as it's called, proceeds by a series of steps such that the output of one step is used as an input for the next one. So let's step out onto our imaginary courtyard and take a look, shall we?

As a starting point, you might imagine your courtyard as being tiled over by two 16- × 16-foot squares, plus a remainder with an area of 6 × 16. To find the size of tile that will work for the whole floor, we need to work on dividing up that remainder.

Fortunately, you can tile two 6- × 6-foot squares in that small space, with an even smaller remainder. This remainder can be once again visualized as a rectangle, this time with an area of 4 × 6. Let's partially fill that with a 4 × 4 square. Now all we have left is a tiny 2 × 4 rectangle. Dividing that with some beautiful sandstone tiles should be easy. We will need just two 2 × 2 tiles. We now have our solution for the entire courtyard. Thinking about the problem mathematically, the greatest common divisor of 16 and 38 is 2. But from a pragmatic standpoint, you can now tell your builder the exact size of tiles to order for your garden to look perfect. He needs to buy 2 × 2 tiles. No number of a larger-sized tile will cover the courtyard without any gaps or overlaps.

The steps of the Euclidean Algorithm can be listed as:

$$38 \div 16 = 2 + 6 \text{ rem}$$
$$16 \div 6 = 2 + 4 \text{ rem}$$
$$6 \div 4 = 1 + 2 \text{ rem}$$
$$4 \div 2 = 2 + 0 \text{ rem}$$

At each step, we take the previous divisor and divide it by the previous remainder, continuing in this way until we get a zero remainder. The figure we have at that step is the GCD.

Of course, there are other algorithmic ways of finding this answer. For instance, we could list the prime factors of each number and then select the factor or factors in common:

$$38 = 2 \times 19$$
$$16 = 2 \times 2 \times 2 \times 2$$

In this case, the GCD is 2.

Don't worry. That's the last math example you will find in this book. I just wanted to illustrate a simple point: algorithms have inputs and outputs. Every step generates a result, which we can then feed as an input to the next step.

When you scale up this idea, algorithms allow us to address very complex, real-world challenges. For example, consider one of the classics of computer science: the Traveling Salesman Problem. The problem goes like this: if a sales representative selling encyclopedias needs to visit multiple locations on a list, what is the shortest possible round trip that goes through each location once without backtracking? Finding the answer is more complex than you might think, and one that logistics companies have to deal with all the time when they try to deliver your parcels in the most efficient way possible. UPS, for example, uses a route optimization tool called ORION (On-Road Integrated Optimization and Navigation) so that drivers can deliver your parcels on time.

Algorithms surround us. When you withdraw money from an ATM, buy something online and have it shipped to your home address, unlock your phone with facial recognition, check your friends' photos on Instagram, browse a personalized playlist on your music service, or select a movie to watch from Netflix's list of recommendations, algorithms are working in the background to anticipate and respond to your needs.

Understand why machines are becoming so smart

While algorithms have been around for thousands of years, the real reason we now live in an algorithmic age is that there have been dramatic advances in deep learning.

With the advent of deep learning, computers can train themselves on datasets that contain millions of inputs and outputs, evolving as they do so. So, instead of repeatedly following a stable set of instructions, like your grandma's recipe for pasta sauce (which you wouldn't dare modify), systems based on machine learning algorithms adapt themselves as they work. Essentially, machines can now write their own instructions.

When did this happen? For some, the turning point was in December 2012, when the team from the University of Toronto won the ImageNet Large-Scale Visual Recognition Challenge competition with their SuperVision algorithm. The ImageNet competition, run since 2010, is an annual software contest that invites teams to develop software programs to correctly classify and detect objects and scenes in images. As their winning entry, Geoffrey Hinton, Alex Krizhevsky, and Ilya Sutskever designed a neural network that they called AlexNet, based on what is known as a deep convolutional neural network.

To put their victory into context, the winning team in 2010 had an error rate of 28.2 per cent. The SuperVision team in 2012 won with an error rate of 16.4 per cent. The next best entry was 26.2 per cent. Since then, the ability of machines to reliably understand images has accelerated dramatically. In 2017, the winning team, from China, had an error rate of only 2.25 per cent. That is probably much better than what you, a highly intelligent human being, could achieve.

A bit like the human brain, AlexNet's convolutional neural network was made up of layers of small neuron collections that each examined a portion of an image, extracting important features. The results from all the collections in a layer were then overlapped to create a representation of an entire image. This was repeated in the layer below, and so on, which allowed the algorithm to understand the contents of an image.

AlexNet helps illustrate the difference between deep learning and general forms of machine learning. In traditional machine learning applications, algorithms are programmed with a defined set of features to look out for. With deep learning, the neural network can define features by analyzing the data that comes from its input layer.

Today, convolutional neural networks are used everywhere and for everything, from automatically tagging your photos, to analyzing video, building and controlling self-driving cars, and drug R&D. But such developments have come about only relatively recently, with the emergence of enough cheap, powerful computation to make deep-learning algorithms a practical tool. As an algorithm, AlexNet was smart; with enough processing power, it could learn to be smarter.

Computers have been a significant part of business design for the last fifty years or so. If they were smart, it was because we programmed them to be that way. The ability of machines to rapidly learn at scale is what makes the algorithmic age radically different from previous ages in which computers also played a key role in processing information and automating transactions. It is only now, because of machine learning, that we face the new reality of computers that can be *smarter than us*.

Concepts like "smart" or "intelligence" can be misleading if not clearly defined. In his book *Life 3.0*, physicist and cosmologist Max Tegmark considers intelligence to be the ability to accomplish complex goals. He defines "complex goals" broadly, encompassing many possible aspects, including understanding, self-awareness, and problem-solving. For Tegmark, the holy grail of AI research is to build an artificial general intelligence (AGI) that is able to accomplish virtually any goal, including learning.

There is another type of AI, however, that you might think of as narrow AI. As Tegmark points out, IBM's Deep Blue chess computer was only able to accomplish the very narrow task of playing chess. It would struggle to succeed in other contexts, even playing other games. You might say that Deep Blue was smart at chess, but when it came to tic-tac-toe, it couldn't even beat a four-year-old.

The founder of Satalia, Daniel Hulme, whom we will meet later in this book, argues that for a machine to be a true AI, it has to exhibit "goal-directed adaptive behavior." Being "goal-directed" refers to the fact that an algorithm is being used to achieve a specific objective, such as classifying an image or optimizing a route. However, the important word here is *adaptive*. In Hulme's view, if a system is not adapting itself, learning from its mistakes, and improving its model, it is not AI; it is just a form of automation.

This ability to adapt, learn, and achieve proficiency within narrow domains is why machines are becoming smarter than us *in specific areas*. In many fields, machines have already surpassed us in our ability not only to play games like chess and Go, but also to spot skin cancers, identify planets, or recognize faces in a crowd. A narrow defined goal, plus the ability to learn, allows today's algorithmic platforms to gain rapid mastery of tasks like pattern recognition, navigation, optimization, or personalization.

In the next few years, we will see an exponential improvement in the abilities of machines to learn. AlphaGo beating the world's best Go player, Lee Sedol, was amazing. But what was truly astounding was its follow-up act, AlphaGo Zero. The "zero" in the name should give you a clue as to how this new AI works: zero human knowledge. Equipped with only the rules of the game and no examples of human games as training data, AlphaGo Zero made random plays until it developed strategies so good that it beat its previous champion-beating incarnation 100–0.

What makes AlphaGo Zero truly interesting is its ability, unlike IBM's Deep Blue chess computer, to apply its learnings to other games. DeepMind, the Google subsidiary that developed AlphaGo, recently reported that it had generalized the software so that it could learn other games. Within twenty-four hours of being unleashed on other games, such as chess and shogi (a Japanese game similar to chess), the AI was able to develop "superhuman skills" and then convincingly defeat a world-champion program. According to DeepMind CEO Demis Hassabis, building an algorithm that can learn without human knowledge allows that algorithm to be applied more easily to multiple real-world problems: "For us AlphaGo wasn't just about winning the game of Go, it was also a big step for us towards building general purpose learning algorithms."

But here is the important part of the story: while machines will get dramatically better at extracting insights from data, spotting patterns, and even making decisions on our behalf, only humans will have the unique ability to imagine innovative ways to use machine intelligence to create experiences, transform organizations, and reinvent the world.

Understanding the ability of today's machines to learn is the first step in imagining the kinds of intelligent platforms that we might build in the future. Predicting the impact of smarter algorithms is more difficult than thinking about the significance of faster or cheaper hardware. We can intuitively imagine the impact of a more powerful computer or a higher-resolution camera. But what is the significance of a more sophisticated algorithm that understands our needs or anticipates our desires? What kinds of industries would a dramatically better speech recognition algorithm (one that worked with all human languages) potentially disrupt? If a machine could accurately gauge human emotions, what new kinds of products and services might be made possible?

The best way to imagine a future shaped by AI is not to focus on machines and their current capabilities, but to think about the potential interactions between algorithms, human behavior, and identity. If you can understand the impact of algorithms on how people live, how they make decisions, and their expectations about how things should work, you can start to design a world for customers who don't even exist yet.

Build for your future customers

When it comes to working backward from the future, there is perhaps no better example than Masayoshi Son. He was born in Japan in 1957, although he didn't stay there very long. He moved to the US when he was sixteen to study at the University of California, Berkeley.

It would have been difficult to be at Berkeley in the mid-1970s and not be infected by the sense that computers were going to change the world. One of Son's fellow students was Bill Joy, who created BSD UNIX while studying there and later founded Sun Microsystems.

It should therefore come as no surprise that when Son returned to Japan in the early '80s, he was inspired to found his own software company, Nihon SoftBank (later shortened to SoftBank). As Japan's computer industry grew, so did SoftBank. Within a few years, Son had secured 50 per cent of the nation's retail market for computer software.

Son's star continued to rise. Despite some misadventures during the first dotcom bust in the early years of the new millennium, which saw him losing about $70 billion (and achieving the dubious distinction of suffering the single most significant loss of personal net worth in human history), Son survived, and SoftBank went on to become Japan's leading broadband provider, the first to bring the iPhone to market, and an early investor in Alibaba.

The latter was particularly important because the $20 million Son bet on Alibaba, then a fledgling Chinese e-commerce company, in 2000 turned into $50 billion when the company went public in 2014. Son's investment may look like an easy decision now, but there was little indication at the time that Jack Ma and his big idea were going to be a success.

I had the opportunity to share a pizza in Hong Kong with Jack Ma and his advisers in the late 1990s, when I was running the Australian operations of Jupiter Research, one of the early competitors of research firms like Gartner and Forrester. My boss and the owner of the company at the time, Alan Meckler, had been approached by Ma's people as a potential investor in his business.

It was an odd lunch, to say the least, and uncomfortable for everyone. Meckler related stories of how his previous investments in China had turned out to be scams. Ma picked at his pizza with a look that suggested he'd rather be anywhere but there. And Ma's advisers were looking at me, wondering what I was even doing at the table.

So, what did Masayoshi Son see in Jack Ma that others had missed? The answer to that lies in how Son makes his strategic bets. He doesn't just invest in companies that he thinks might someday be successful or profitable; instead, he forms a very personal view of what the future might look like and works backward from there.

On a recent trip to Tokyo, I met Akira Tada, one of the senior VPs of SoftBank's business in Japan. I was curious about SoftBank's Vision Fund, which has raised $93 billion since its launch in late 2016 to invest in the future. Tada was responsible for one of the fund's latest investments, Plenty, an indoor agriculture business.

When the founder of Plenty pitched SoftBank for an investment, he explained that the two most significant uncontrollable variables in the agriculture business were human labor and the weather. Plenty planned to minimize the impact of both through the use of AI, automation, and controlled internal environments. The plan was to build vertical farms near cities of at least 1 million people.

The idea struck a chord with Son because he was working on a blueprint of what life might be like in 2050. Son is exceptional at long-term thinking and planning. Through intense research and reflection, he builds a picture of what life might be like in thirty years. He then asks himself what technologies, business models, and infrastructure might therefore need to be in place in fifteen years, ten years, five years, and next year. Then, with a singular focus, whenever he encounters an opportunity, business, or individual that fits with his vision, he pursues it relentlessly.

Not surprisingly, such dedication to future vision has implications for the operating model at SoftBank. You can't have a traditional budgeting function when you are working on extended timescales in new markets with a high degree of unpredictability. Tada explained that working at SoftBank means accepting a more responsive approach to decision making and strategy. Son, he said, frequently quips, "If it's raining, open an umbrella." In other words, if the investment company is losing a certain amount of money, cut expenses by a specified amount. If after a year it is still losing money, cut 30 per cent, for example, of staff and then continue as normal. Son might not know precisely when his vision of the future will become reality, but he is confident of one thing: he needs to ensure that his companies are around long enough for it to happen.

Not everyone has the luxury of billions to invest in companies and sectors that may not eventuate for decades. However, shifting your focus from keeping your current customers happy to thinking about what your future customers might want will ensure that you start to solve problems today that your competitors won't be thinking about until tomorrow. It is no mystery who these customers are. Chances are, you have already met some of them.

Learn from your kids

If you want to design products and services that will thrive in the future, you have to focus on the people who will live in it. Your customers of 2030 are alive today. They are your children and grandchildren. They are eight years old or younger—and they think completely differently than you.

For anyone born after 2007, the most significant influence in their childhood was that slender, touch screen phone Steve Jobs brought into the world in that year. Like me, you have probably been both fascinated and horrified by watching babies using sophisticated pieces of technology.

In 2015, a team of University of Iowa researchers decided to analyze more than 200 YouTube videos, which they used as a source of insight into how young children were using tablets. They discovered that by age two, 90 per cent of the children in the videos had a moderate ability to use a tablet. They defined "moderate ability" as needing help from an adult to access apps, but being able to use them while displaying some difficulty with basic interactions. Even toddlers, when exposed to technology, can do something meaningful with it. So, what does that mean for their future?

Most of us, when dealing with young kids in the modern world, have probably struggled with how to moderate their use of technology. The struggle is an important one, because as one researcher discovered, it holds the key to our children's future success.

Over the last few years, researcher Alexandra Samuel has been gathering data on how more than 10,000 parents in North America have been managing the challenges of raising kids in a digital world. In doing so, she uncovered three distinct digital parenting styles.

The first group of parents she called *digital enablers*. These parents allow their kids to manage their own technology use, with lots of access to devices and screen time, if the kids so desire. *Digital limiters*, by contrast, are parents who will use the off switch, restricting technology use for fear of the potential impact on their children's attention spans and how they interact with others. The final group are *digital mentors*, who take an active role in guiding their kids in the digital world.

Mentors, in her view, may be the parents who are most successful in preparing their kids for the algorithmic age, not only working actively to shape their kids' online skills and experiences but also connecting with them through technology.

Ultimately, these differences in parenting will, according to Samuel, lead to three separate groups in the upcoming generations: *digital orphans, digital exiles,* and *digital heirs*. The digital orphans, those who had unfettered access to technology, will struggle with interpersonal connections. The digital exiles, having been shielded from the Internet, will lack the skills to make good choices, and perhaps worse, the capabilities to be successful in a data-driven work environment. That leaves the digital heirs, who may be best placed to mediate between real and virtual environments, and as a result, will excel in the algorithmic age.

When I interviewed Samuel for this book, she told me a story about her own kids, and one of her proudest moments as a parent: "Both my kids got their first Gmail accounts within the same year, each of them without any prompting from me, and without them knowing what the other had done," she began, before continuing with a warm laugh.

"The first email that my eldest sent was just the words 'magic wand,' 'magic wand,' 'magic wand' over and over again, while my youngest's first email was 'toy robot,' 'toy robot,' 'toy robot.' Each of my kids had spontaneously done this for the same reason. They knew that Gmail spies on your email and uses it to serve ads. My eldest wanted to see toys for a magic wand, and my youngest wanted to see ads for toy robots, and so they each had that same idea. With their first email, they would engineer it to give them the ads that they wanted."

"So they had already developed a mental model for the machine learning algorithm that Google was using?" I asked.

"Exactly, and they were only seven and ten years old at the time."

"I didn't know where you were going to go with the end of your story," I said. "I honestly thought you were going to say they were trying to write to Santa."

"Give me a break. Who needs Santa when you've got the algorithm, right? Santa's for losers who don't know how to use Gmail to serve them the ads they want."

Samuel's story provides another useful clue for understanding your future customers, and it has to do with how her two kids were able to form a mental model of an algorithm they were exposed to and use that model to achieve their own ends. This new generation, those born after 2007, is the first not only to have had access to smartphones from birth, but also to have been completely immersed in algorithmic platforms. Merely being exposed to that many algorithms changes the way you think and how you see the world.

Take a moment to think about your own household. There is probably a smart speaker in your living room that can provide your kids with answers to all their questions that you might be too tired or distracted to answer. On their smartphones are apps for videos, music, and entertainment that algorithmically adjust themselves to their behavior and preferences. Even when they access Instagram or Facebook, the feeds that serve up messages, pictures, and updates about their social circle are personalized just for them, with an uncanny ability to anticipate and even influence their interests and behavior. We think of all these technologies as AI, but for your kids, it's more like an imaginary friend, or perhaps even an additional parent.

In a nutshell, what your kids already know, and what you are perhaps only now beginning to realize, is that the most interesting thing about the future will not be new devices or gadgets, but what happens next with our algorithmic experiences.

Focus on experiences, not devices

Here's the story of how Steve Jobs tricked you.

When Jobs delivered his keynote address at the Macworld Conference & Expo in 2007, he pretended to be introducing three products: a widescreen iPod with touch controls, a revolutionary mobile phone, and a breakthrough Internet communications device. You know the ending, of course: these were not three separate devices; they were one device, and he called it an iPhone.

But Jobs's real trick was yet to come. Although the iPhone was sold to us as a convergence of disparate pieces of hardware, it actually led to a *divergence* of devices from algorithmic experiences. Smartphones were great, but the new world of mobile apps that they made possible was truly amazing. These apps were more than just pieces of software; they were algorithmic platforms that had a life beyond just your phone, working seamlessly across whatever platform, device, or operating system you happened to be using.

When you trust your music experiences to Spotify, your relationship to that platform is not limited by your hardware. Aside from your smartphone, you can listen to your playlists in your car, on your home stereo, on your laptop, or even on someone else's phone. The same applies to almost all of your algorithmic experiences, whether it be the way you watch TV shows, share photos, talk to your friends, or manage your transportation. Your algorithmic experience transcends your devices.

We are just entering a new age of algorithmic experiences that will be fueled by exponential advances in machine intelligence. AI has the potential to transform the way we interact with the world, but it will be your job as an algorithmic leader to imagine what that future might look like and figure out how we get there.

A useful way to start designing algorithmic experiences is by thinking about the relationships between intentions, interactions, and identity.

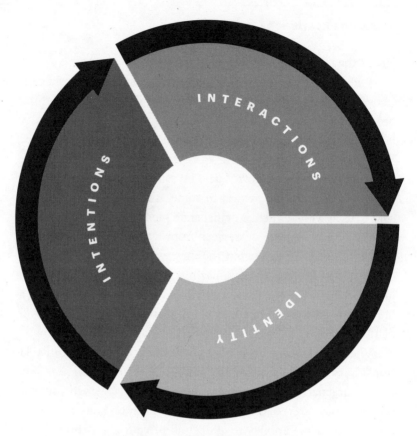

The Wheel of Algorithmic Experience

Intentions are the often unarticulated needs or desires of a user or customer, which can be deduced from their behavior. *Interactions* are the method or manner by which you use a platform, product, or service. *Identity* is the cognitive or emotional impact of the experience and the degree to which it has become integrated into a participant's sense of self.

All three elements are connected and self-reinforcing, like a flywheel: anticipating a user's *intentions* allows you to create more natural *interactions*, such that the system itself becomes an extension of their *identity*. And the more an algorithm influences someone's behavior, the more it can anticipate their future intentions, making interactions more effortless, and so on.

The true measure of success for an algorithmic experience is that you stop noticing the algorithm altogether. In other words, it can be considered successful when it disappears. When this happens, searching on Google becomes your transactive memory system, your Instagram feed becomes the collective narrative of your social circle, and Spotify's recommended songs become your musical taste.

There is danger in this. Like video games or slot machines, algorithmic experiences can be designed to manipulate human behavior by weaponizing the reward loops in our brain that lead to addiction. That's not to say that all algorithmic experiences are evil; it is just that any time you are dealing with systems that learn to be progressively better at influencing your behavior, the risk for abuse is high. We will explore the ethics of those issues later in this book, but for now, let's focus on the machinery by which algorithmic experiences operate.

Intentions

When asked why he always wore the same style of gray T-shirt every day, Mark Zuckerberg replied that he wanted to simplify his life so that he could make as few decisions as possible. Steve Jobs wore the same style of black turtleneck daily, and Barack Obama the same gray or blue suit. All these leaders adopted this approach to help cut back on the cognitive fatigue of having to make too many decisions.

As humans, we face constant decisions. Not just what we wear, but also what we buy, what we eat, where we go, whom we talk to, and what we should pay attention to. It has been estimated that an adult might make around 35,000 decisions every single day. Researchers at Cornell University discovered that we make 226.7 daily decisions about food alone. The constant pressure to make choices creates stress. Psychologist Barry Schwartz, author of *The Paradox of Choice*, has talked about how too much choice can create a sense of paralysis and dissatisfaction.

Your kids are unlikely to be in that position, given that an increasing number of their choices are being automated for them. Once you have experienced a world where your decisions are handled for you by smart algorithms, there is no going back. Algorithms and data make "anticipatory design" possible. Anticipatory design in interfaces and applications is premised on the idea that if you can reliably predict what a user wants, it is better to limit the number of choices offered to them.

Consider the Google Now app, which attempts to answer your questions and solve your issues before you've even had to think about them: if you have an upcoming meeting or a restaurant booking, it will suggest travel time based on your current location and traffic. Or think about the Nest thermostat, which will adjust the temperature of the room you are in, based on your behavior and the temperature-related decisions you have made previously. In a similar vein, Netflix doesn't show you all the movies in its catalog, just the ones it believes you might want to watch. And if you don't like its suggestions, it will offer you different ones to pick from the next time you visit.

When Amazon obtained a patent for "anticipatory shipping" in 2014, people's imaginations started to run wild. Would Amazon, based on what it knew about your behavior and intentions, start sending you packages without your placing an order? Not quite. The patent described a method by which Amazon would preemptively box and ship items that it predicted its customers in a specific area might want. These items would then wait in small, strategically placed warehouses—or even on trucks—until the anticipated order actually arrived. This would allow Amazon to send you replacement dishwashing liquid or paper towels almost as soon as you told Alexa that you had run out.

The fact that Amazon had been thinking of such an idea as early as 2014 illustrates just how seriously they take the idea of algorithmically anticipating customer intentions. It is not enough to meet a customer request when it is asked. In an age of algorithmic experiences, anticipating what someone may want without their having to ask will be the new normal.

Interactions

Your kids may have grown up with smartphones, but that doesn't mean they will expect everything to work on small screens in the future. Like me, you probably embarked on your digital experience by typing computer commands from a DOS prompt. I doubt you would be impressed if someone asked you to use that kind of interface today.

The next big shift in interface design is the move toward more natural interactions. Our bodies are becoming interfaces. Whether it be smart speakers or sensors, smart tattoos or augmented reality glasses, we are learning to sense and respond to data in a more intuitive way. The more natural the interface, the more likely we are to start forgetting about the algorithmic machinery hard at work in the background.

Facial recognition, for example, has rapidly become the default way that people authenticate themselves on digital platforms in China. If you ran in the Shanghai International Half Marathon in the spring of 2018, you might have uploaded a selfie to the PaoBu WeiShengSu official account on WeChat (also known as Weixin). Within a few moments of doing so, a filtering system with a facial recognition algorithm would have provided you with a multitude of photos of you, automatically curated, and taken by thousands of freelance photographers who covered the race. The watermarked photos were free, and the clean shots were available for purchase.

Didi Chuxing, the Uber of China, uses facial recognition technology to check the identity of its drivers before they start a trip.

China Construction Bank allows customers to pay with their faces at some vending machines. A growing number of police officers are equipped with augmented reality glasses that allow them to scan crowds and look for suspects. Even the Temple of Heaven in Beijing has started using facial recognition technology to address the regular theft of toilet paper. The paper dispenser recognizes faces and cuts you off after frequent repeat visits (the disaster potential of this isn't hard to imagine).

The sheer scale of the digital world in China, the amount of data that their local platforms can collect, and their ability to use this data to train ever-improving algorithms mean that what happens in China will determine the fate of algorithmic systems everywhere. Hundreds of millions of people use WeChat, a platform that started as a chat service and has grown to become a kind of operating system for daily life. WeChat facilitates the purchase of everything from food and clothing, to insurance and financial products. Similarly, Didi Chuxing, a transportation platform, is massive—and growing rapidly. It has 450 million registered users and 21 million drivers, and provides over 25 million rides per day. Uber, by contrast, provided less than half that worldwide per day in 2017.

All of this data is likely to be amalgamated by the Chinese government as part of their Social Credit System, a national reputation system designed to determine the "trustworthiness" of the country's 1.4 billion citizens. In this new prototype algorithmic society, your ability to buy train tickets, attend good schools, access health services, or even find a match on dating apps will depend on your good behavior, your viewpoints, and whether you follow the rules.

As they collect more and more data from our interactions, tomorrow's digital platforms will do a better job of understanding our intentions and responding rapidly to our unarticulated desires. We will talk rather than type, smile rather than swipe. Instead of automation creating more standardized experiences, your future customers will expect you to leverage machine learning to create more natural, personalized, human-level interactions.

However, there is a fine line between useful and unsettling. Google Duplex, for example, is a new AI technology that uses natural conversations to carry out tasks like scheduling appointments over the phone. People called by the service can speak normally, just as they would to another person, without having to adapt their speech to be recognizable to a machine. In fact, it is not even obvious that you are talking to a machine. And that, for many, was the most disconcerting aspect of the demo of the product.

At the launch, Google's director of Augmented Intelligence Research, Greg Corrado, explained that over the next decade he expected to see the development of artificial emotional intelligence that will allow products to actually have much more natural and fluid human interactions. The most shocking moment was when, in response to a question from a human on the other end of the phone, the algorithmic voice paused and said "hmmm" before continuing. According to a Google blog post, this was deliberate. The system was designed to sound more natural via the incorporation of typical speech disfluencies and fillers (e.g., *hmmms* and *aaahs*) to mimic what people often do when they are gathering their thoughts. But is this a good idea?

There is a difference between creating natural interfaces that are human-level and don't require us to modify our behavior to use them, and tricking people into thinking they are engaging with a human. Think of it as the difference between human-level and human-like. Human-like interfaces often risk failing the uncanny valley test, a term coined in 1970 by a Japanese robotics professor named Masahiro Mori.

Mori argued that as the appearance of a robot becomes more human-like, our emotional response to the robot becomes increasingly positive and empathetic, but there is a point at which our response quickly turns to strong revulsion. However, as the robot starts to become harder to distinguish from a real human, our emotional response then starts to become positive again and our empathy levels approach those we would display toward another human.

While Google may very well succeed in creating an interface that is indistinguishable from a human, the real question is, *should it?* In the future, we may insist that AIs identify to the user that they are machines and not humans. Human-like interfaces that attempt to simulate, imitate, and ultimately deceive us into thinking they are humans may engender distrust, suspicion, and even fear.

Human-level interfaces that understand our natural speech, recognize our faces, respond to our emotional states, and even track our gestures will be useful. They will allow us to effortlessly communicate our intentions and accomplish our objectives without resorting to command interfaces and workflows. And in doing so, we may start to see algorithms as an extension of ourselves.

Identity

When algorithms become deeply embedded in our daily lives, they have the potential to greatly influence how we behave. If we reach that point, we will no longer be able to easily discern how much of our memory, experiences, tastes, or even our own identity is native to us and how much is merely the technological extensions of ourselves.

To see how algorithms could play such a large role in shaping our behavior, you need to understand the rapid growth of the Internet of Things (IoT), the vast interconnected network of devices, vehicles, appliances, sensors, and wearables that is estimated to total 30 billion devices by 2020.

Some of these IoT devices are industrial, connecting sensors at manufacturing facilities or car engines with race crews. However, many more are consumer-oriented in nature. They are the devices that we wear on our wrists, around our necks, in our clothing, and soon enough, on our skin and inside our bodies. These devices will provide an opportunity for companies and brands to directly influence and shape how we think, feel, and act.

Knowing how you want people to behave is not the same as knowing what you want people to pay attention to. Most marketers are focused on monitoring whether or not their brand messages reach their intended audiences. They focus on click-throughs, interactions, and brand recall. However, if you could embed everything we know about how people behave—and why—into the design and deployment of smart devices, your marketing department might need to shift its focus to *What do we want our customer to do next?*

How and why people make decisions, especially in relation to money and investments, has become an area of intense study for economists and cognitive researchers alike. In 2017, economist Richard Thaler won the Nobel Memorial Prize in Economic Sciences for his contributions to behavioral economics and his work in establishing that people are predictably irrational in ways that defy economic theory. These insights have already been applied in government and by multiple companies to shift or nudge people's behavior.

A "nudge" is a strategy employed to change someone's behavior, sometimes referred to as "non-enforced compliance." In their 2008 book, *Nudge: Improving Decisions about Health, Wealth, and Happiness*, Thaler and Cass Sunstein demonstrated that by designing the choice architecture (the way in which options are presented) differently, you can influence people toward making a specific choice without restrictions, prohibitions, or a change in costs.

Technology companies have long been experimenting with choice architecture on not only their users but also their own employees. Google, for example, famous for providing a wide variety of perks for employees in their offices, grew concerned that its employees were eating too much unhealthy food and drinking high-calorie sodas. Rather than restricting candy and cola, it decided to put healthy snacks in clear jars that were easy to reach and place the water at eye level in the fridge. Within the first seven weeks of trialing this approach, the drop in M&M consumption among employees in Google's New York office alone translated into 3.1 million fewer calories being ingested.

Our devices can also nudge us to behave in different ways. Many of us wear smartwatches that can remind us to drink more water, breathe, stand up, or take more steps. Soon our refrigerators will keep track of what we eat, our toilets will report on our physical health, or our shoes will vibrate to alert us to walk in the direction of something we might find personally interesting.

From one perspective, our growing reliance on algorithms to make decisions can be seen as a dangerous loss of personal autonomy. An alternative view is that we are witnessing the emergence of a new, symbiotic relationship with technology that allows us to augment and extend our five senses. Just as geese can sense the Earth's geomagnetic field and use it to navigate, the next generation of humans may start to develop a kind of "data sense" that will influence and shape their behavior in a multitude of ways.

Even without dedicated devices to nudge their users, platforms will also need to think strategically about the kinds of behaviors that optimize their network's overall value. Tinder, the dating application, provides an interesting example. There is a concept in competitive chess, known as an Elo score, that is used to assess and rank each player's skill. Tinder has its own Elo score, which it uses to rate your attractiveness.

In the world of chess, if a low-ranked player beats a high-ranked one, that low-ranked player gets a better Elo score, and so forth. Similarly, if a user with a high Elo score on Tinder swipes right and likes someone with a lower score, the lower-ranked user gets an increase in their score. However, Tinder's algorithm is complex and also takes into account other behavioral indicators, such as how quickly people respond to messages, whether they are selective in whom they like, and other actions that are deemed consistent with Tinder's optimal usage model.

The curious part of these algorithmic systems is that they are not always completely transparent in their workings, which leads to an entire online community of speculation and information sharing with a view to gaming or hacking the system. Just like Alexandra Samuel's kids, we too may be tempted to type "magic wand" or "toy robot" on our screens, if we think that by doing so, we can make them appear.

Part of the challenge of designing future platforms is not only figuring how you want people to behave, but also being able to constantly adapt and adjust to the collective knowledge of users who try to manipulate your algorithms and game the system.

Although much of this chapter has focused on explaining what algorithms are, the real takeaway concerns what matters in the future. As you start to pull together your vision for where the world might go, remember to center your perspective on future customer behavior. In the long term, the real driver of business value will be the ways that algorithms and AI can create compelling customer experiences.

SUMMARY

1 By understanding algorithms and how they shape our interactions and experiences as human beings, you can gain insight into the kinds of data-driven platforms and products that are likely to succeed in the future.

2 Unlike the platforms of the previous digital revolution, today's machines are starting to teach themselves, and in doing so, they are gaining levels of mastery that match or surpass human beings'

abilities in specific fields or activities. Humans, however, are still in the driver's seat when it comes to imagining ways to use machine intelligence to create experiences, transform organizations, and reinvent the world.

3 Algorithmic leaders can prepare for the future by understanding who their future customers are and what they might want. Masayoshi Son, CEO of SoftBank, is an example of an algorithmic leader who starts with a strong vision of the future and works backward from there.

4 Your kids are the forerunner generation of the algorithmic age. Having grown up surrounded by AI embedded in all their products and applications, they will have a radically different set of expectations and perspectives about the way that the world should work. Learn from them.

5 The greatest driver of business value in the future will not be the algorithms that you use to optimize your operations and infrastructure, but those that create compelling experiences for your customers and clients. Use the Wheel of Algorithmic Experience—intentions, interactions, and identity—to imagine how algorithms might respond to what your customers want, as well as how they behave and see themselves.

QUESTION

What is more valuable: knowing who your best customers are, or identifying the ideal behaviors that maximize the value of your platform or service?

2

AIM FOR 10X, NOT 10%

"I have no intention of making small bets."
MASAYOSHI SON, CEO OF SOFTBANK

Focus on multiples, not margins

While leaders worry about the impact of disruptive ideas on their business or industry, what they should really be worrying about is whether their own ideas are disruptive enough.

If you are simply automating your existing processes, adding a chatbot to your website, or updating your mobile app, then in all probability you are not thinking big enough about your future opportunities. Too often, *digital transformation* is just *digital incrementalism.*

When you invest in new technology but stop short of challenging your business model out of fear of a more radical transformation, you are merely delaying the inevitable moment when everything changes and you are caught out. Part of the journey to becoming an algorithmic leader is being brave enough to pursue opportunities that deliver results in multiples, not just margins.

I met Reid Hoffman, founder of LinkedIn, in the early 2000s, when the company was only a few years old and its office in Mountain View still had that magical atmosphere of a startup on the brink of rapid growth. Hoffman was friendly, incisive, and without a doubt one of the smartest people I've ever met in Silicon Valley.

The thing I remember most clearly from our meeting was Hoffman's advice about growth. Hoffman explained that he only started or invested in companies that had a built-in, network growth model. If a company relied on traditional advertising to grow, it wasn't for him. He sought opportunities that leveraged data, computation, and user networks to expand rapidly and thus gain a competitive advantage.

The only thing worse than a lack of growth is the opportunity cost of not growing fast enough. When you have gained enough scale, you can approach the structure of your organization, the design of your platforms, and the dynamics of your industry in a completely different way.

Hoffman refined his network growth concept into something he calls *Blitzscaling*. His idea was that startups were in a race to get to the point in their life cycle when the most value could be created. Take too long, and either your competitors overtake you or you drain yourself of the resources you need to survive. Basically, you need to go straight from "startup" to "scale up."

Similarly, being an algorithmic leader means thinking differently about the strategic opportunities that you pursue, and the speed with which you pursue them. Whereas a leader from the analogue era might have won acclaim by achieving small gains in operating margins through being disciplined about pricing, holding less inventory, or taking longer to pay suppliers, an algorithmic leader needs to think big just to survive.

When a venture capitalist says they need 10× returns on their investment, it sounds greedy until you understand that investing in startups is inherently risky and many don't work out as expected. In fact, many early-stage investors assume that one-third of their investments will fail completely, one-third will barely return the money invested, and the remaining third will pay off.

However, the real reason algorithmic leaders need to think in multiples is not because of business risk but because twenty-first-century industries based on data and algorithms tend to operate in a "winner-takes-all" market.

If you wanted to start a search engine today to compete with Google, it would not be sufficient to deliver a marginal improvement in search query time or a local market offering. You have to offer the scale, data, machine learning algorithms, and technology infrastructure to provide a comprehensive solution for everyone—if you don't, you can't provide a good service for anyone.

That's not to say that operational efficiency is not a worthy objective. Domino's Pizza, for example, is experimenting with an AI camera system designed to automatically check for quality. It can tell the difference between various types of pizza and also determine if pizzas are at the proper temperature. Similarly, Coca-Cola uses an algorithm called the Black Book model that combines data from satellite imagery, weather patterns, expected crop yields, cost pressures, and consumer preferences to produce a consistent-tasting orange juice all year round. The issue here is still scale. The more your products or processes can improve through data and algorithmic learning, the harder it will be for new and small entrants to compete against you.

One of the founding concepts at Amazon is the "flywheel of growth." The logic goes like this: a wider selection of products and services at lower prices leads to more traffic that in turn leads to more customers and sales, which supports the expansion into new categories of products and services, and so on. Amazon's flywheel is about more than just the benefits of customer momentum; it describes the advantages that you gain with a critical mass of data and algorithmic models. If you can structure your organization around learning models built on data loops, you will create a reinforcing cycle. More data leads to better models, which makes your products and processes better, and so on.

By thinking bigger about your algorithmic opportunities, and engineering a platform for more than you need today, you can potentially shift from a linear growth model to an exponential one.

Don't let a great idea hold you back from a better one

Great ideas can be the foundation of a great business, but they can also hold you back if you let them. You need to be flexible enough to allow new ideas to replace the old. Sometimes that means nothing more than a change in structure. But sometimes, it means a change in people.

In early May 2013, then Microsoft CEO Steve Ballmer was finishing a morning run on a London street. Taking a few minutes to catch his breath, he reflected on his last few months at Microsoft.

The company, himself included, was under immense pressure to change. The board and key shareholders were demanding a new management structure and a renewed focus on mobile devices and online services.

Ballmer's revelation that morning was that Microsoft might change faster without him as CEO. "At the end of the day, we need to break a pattern," he explained in an interview to the *Wall Street Journal*. "Face it: I'm a pattern."

Windows was a great idea—and one that almost destroyed Microsoft. When a company's product has powerful momentum, it can blind leaders to new opportunities as they arise. Great ideas can become like scar tissue that protects the organization from the outside but ultimately compromises its capacity to be flexible, adapt, and change. Great ideas from the past can keep you looking for marginal improvements in the present, while missing the opportunity for more radical transformation.

During Ballmer's reign as CEO, revenue at Microsoft tripled to almost $78 billion in the year ending June 2013, and profit grew 132 per cent to nearly $22 billion. But even as enterprises renewed their software licenses and consumers bought PCs with Windows products installed on them, the company made critical mistakes, such as underestimating the potential impact of the Web and so being late in releasing their own browser, delaying their entry to the search engine advertising market and the digital music ecosystem, and almost completely missing the consumer shift to mobile devices and social media. By 2013, Microsoft was on the verge of missing an even bigger transformation in the nature of software itself: the shift from physical software distribution to cloud-based subscriptions.

Ballmer is a classic analogue-era leader. He grew up in Detroit and was a college football coach when he met Bill Gates. He dropped out of his MBA studies to become Microsoft's first business manager. At a time when growth in the computer software business was all about aggressive sales and market share expansion, he helped build a competitive culture of corporate silos, where colleagues were measured and pitted against each other. While this created a competitive spirit that drove performance when Windows was king, it later made it difficult for leaders to come together when the dynamics of the industry changed and the company needed to evolve.

When Satya Nadella was appointed as the new leader of the company in 2014, he realized that Microsoft had built a rigid capability and culture around Windows. Even as Windows as a product became less relevant, the company had failed to develop new functional capabilities. Nadella quickly shifted Microsoft's focus to cloud computing, artificial intelligence, and social networking. However, the most important change he introduced would be the way that the company thought about itself.

When interviewed by McKinsey & Company for a podcast, Nadella explained it was natural for the core product of a company to begin to stagnate at some point. That's when you needed new capabilities to stimulate the creation and growth of new concepts and products. In his view, in a time of constant and rapid change, an innovative corporate culture enables you to keep trying out new concepts before they become the norm.

What makes Nadella's approach both powerful and pragmatic is how he distinguishes between capabilities and business units. When companies do well, they tend to organize by business units. They do this because they believe it will provide efficiency, productivity, and lower transaction costs. Unfortunately, technology companies are driven by capability rather than structure.

To chase new 10× opportunities, you can't rely on your traditional silos and functional departments. Even if you know where the future of your business might be, getting there requires a more agile approach—in other words, allowing your teams and leaders to quickly adjust their plans, projects, responsibilities, and even job titles without adhering to rigid organizational structures and approval processes.

Learn to follow the data

Given that the house always wins, it seems improbable that a casino could go broke. Strangely enough, that is exactly what happened in 2015 when Caesars filed for bankruptcy protection, weighed down by $24 billion of debt. One of the most fascinating details of those proceedings was a complaint made by the creditors, who argued that there was an item in Caesars' asset list that had been grossly undervalued. In their view, the most valuable thing that Caesars owned was not its real estate or their brands, but its data. The creditors argued that the Total Rewards customer data program, made up of seventeen years of data on some 45 million program members, should have been valued at US$1 billion.

Caesars is not unique in this respect. Your organization's current most valuable asset is your data. And its value is only set to grow. To understand why, you have to appreciate the special significance data plays in the world of algorithms and AI.

Geoffrey Hinton, Alex Krizhevsky, and Ilya Sutskever did not use neural networks as part of their winning strategy in the 2012 ImageNet challenge by chance. Hinton was persuaded to use the technique by a young Stanford college professor and computer prodigy named Andrew Ng.

Growing up in Asia, Ng learned to code at a young age from his father, a doctor who even made an enthusiastic attempt to program a computer system to diagnose his patients. Ng was no ordinary teenager. By sixteen, he had already figured out how to use neural networks to help solve math problems.

After graduating from high school, Ng studied at three institutions famed for their computer science programs—Carnegie Mellon, MIT, and Berkeley—before becoming a professor at Stanford University. When graphics chip maker NVIDIA made its graphics processing units (GPUs) designed for gaming available for general purposes in 2007, Ng and his research team at Stanford quickly realized that the chips could also be used to supercharge neural networks.

Until this point, computer scientists typically relied on general-purpose processors, like the ones made by Intel that sat inside consumer PCs, in order to execute algorithms. Although fast, conventional computer chips can only manage a few computational tasks at any one time, and neural networks require the capability to run thousands of calculations at the same time. Fortunately, chips that could meet that need did exist. They were designed for video games, and the best ones were made by NVIDIA.

So, newly armed with cheap processing power in the form of GPUs, Ng started publishing papers on deep learning at a prodigious rate. It was these papers that inspired the University of Toronto's winning approach in 2012, kicking off a renaissance in AI based on deep learning and neural networks.

However, it wasn't long before Ng realized he would need even more computational power so he could take his research further. That led him to Google, and with access to that company's vast computing power and data, he formed the Google Brain initiative in 2011. One of his team's most interesting experiments was to use YouTube as an unsupervised training dataset for a machine learning algorithm. Ng's system famously learned to identify what a cat looked like, without having to be told to look for one, or even knowing what a cat was.

In 2014, Ng accepted an offer to join Chinese Web giant Baidu after it announced it would invest $300 million in a new research-and-development center in Silicon Valley. Not surprisingly, the first thing Ng did after joining Baidu was to purchase a lot of GPUs. Part of his role at Baidu was to identify and resource projects that could leverage AI effectively across a wide range of industries and applications.

His experience at Baidu ultimately led the machine learning pioneer to strike out on his own, and he eventually set up a

US$175 million AI fund. In a blog post explaining his decision, Ng equated the development of AI with the rise of electricity. In the early days of electricity, he wrote, much of the innovation focused on coming up with slightly different improvements on lighting, which was its original application. The really transformative applications, in which electric power led to the reshaping of entire industries, took much longer to be harnessed. In his view, AI is the electricity of the twenty-first century.

Ng believes companies should put data at their heart of their business. Finding the right data to train machine learning algorithms is not easy, not least because the data is often held by protective incumbent players. At Baidu, Ng often designed and launched applications with the specific goal of acquiring particular datasets that targeted an aspect of user behavior or a geographic region. He had learned that to get somewhere interesting, first you have to follow the data.

When you look at the career path of an algorithmic leader like Ng, you find a commitment to looking for the bigger idea. Finding the 10× opportunity requires not only computer power and financial resources, but also rich and interesting datasets for your algorithms to learn from. For Ng, data is more than an asset. Data should drive your strategy.

Unlock the value of your own knowledge

The importance of data in fueling AI and machine learning creates a unique opportunity for traditional companies that already have a lot of it. If you are looking for your next big idea, chances are that the foundation for it may lie in your own data.

Large, established companies have spent years gathering data on their customers, customers' interactions with suppliers and partners, and the performance of their own platforms and operating units. Of course, that data is rarely in a form easily parsed by algorithms, but simply having access to it is a powerful asset that new entrants to the market lack. What large companies tend to lack, however, is the incentive to use their data trove in interesting ways.

To paraphrase Andrew Ng, just because an aging shopping mall builds a new website it doesn't mean it can become an e-commerce company ready to take on Amazon.

There are no shortcuts to becoming an algorithmic organization. Given the value of your data, the first step is to centralize your information in one place—virtually. Walmart, for example, the world's biggest retailer with over 20,000 stores in twenty-eight countries, is in the process of building the world's biggest private cloud to process 2.5 petabytes of data every hour. That data facility will give them the unprecedented ability to find patterns and correlations in their customer and operational data that will allow them to make dramatic changes to their operating model and potentially launch entirely new ventures.

Sometimes called a "data lake," this first stage of digital transformation requires a coordinated approach to data management and a solid analytics platform. Pooling data from disparate systems is not enough. Algorithmic leaders also need to think carefully about data availability, data acquisition, data labeling, and data governance. You are not just tidying up your data, after all; you are trying to become an organization where data is the primary product that you create and nurture.

According to Richard Socher, the chief scientist at Salesforce, getting data right is a serious engineering challenge. It requires integrating data from different places, cleaning and labeling it, organizing appropriate hardware infrastructure, balancing loads, obtaining good documentation for developers, and only then thinking about trust, security, and permission schemes.

For leaders working in large organizations, that all requires both planning and creativity. Funding a lab to do fundamental research is not enough. That was a mistake that technology companies like Microsoft made for many years—their academics consistently came up with brilliant ideas that couldn't be commercialized. To create an algorithmic organization, you need to figure out how to bring together your engineering and product teams to create entirely new ways of working and identify the parts of your business that might benefit most from AI.

A good example is how Rolls-Royce, the manufacturer of the world's best jet engines, launched an initiative it called R2 Data Labs. The idea was to create interdisciplinary teams of data experts and leaders from various areas throughout Rolls-Royce operations to create new AI-centric services or unlock operational efficiencies. The plan is to build a virtual copy of every engine Rolls-Royce makes, combining data insights from throughout the business with design and manufacturing data, resulting in a perfect *digital twin* of their underlying physical asset.

If you can unlock the value of your own knowledge, you can then use it as a platform to launch disruptive new ideas. For example, MassMutual, a traditional life insurance company, wanted to find a way to reinvent the customer experience of buying insurance by offering instant approvals online. To do so, it created a new company that it called Haven Life. Aside from financial support from its parent company, Haven Life had one important asset that no other startup in the insurance space could match: it had access to Mass-Mutual's historical data, which comprised 1 million policies going back about fifteen years.

Typically, applying for a life insurance product requires a lot of paperwork and analysis. This is because life insurance relies on actuarial data, which is the grim science of predicting how long someone will live. To correlate with actuarial models and generate a predicted lifespan, customers typically see a doctor, undergo a medical exam and blood tests, and answer a long list of medical history questions. Rather than subject its online customers to this process, Haven Life was able to use machine learning and data on the correlations between previous policy holders and their lifespans to allow it to predict an applicant's risk profile—all without resorting to the time-consuming, paper-heavy traditional process.

Data and algorithms offer traditional companies a chance to reinvent themselves. The more provocative question, however, is whether we still need the company itself in the twenty-first century.

Imagine a future without your company in it

Companies as a concept have been around for a long time. While the earliest records of a joint stock company date back to China during the Song Dynasty (AD 960–1279), probably the most famous template of a global corporation is that of the East India Company. Granted an English Royal Charter by Elizabeth I on December 31, 1600, that provided it with a fifteen-year monopoly on all trade in the East Indies, the East India Company became not only the first but perhaps the most infamous example of a public/private partnership, as it transformed from a commercial trading venture to a semi-governmental and military organization that expanded to rule over India and exploit its resources.

But is this traditional idea of a company—one limited by shares and that employs hundreds or even thousands of people full time— still an adequate reflection of our new world, driven as it is by data and algorithms? For example, could you design a company that had no people in it and that existed as nothing more than lines of code? If an AI were to design an organization optimized for machine learning, how would that company operate?

The classic rationale for the existence of a company comes from the pioneering work of a young undergraduate named Ronald Coase, who in the early twentieth century dared to ask, "Why do companies exist?"

In 1931, at age twenty, Coase left England to travel around the United States, interviewing entrepreneurs and economists. Lenin had boasted that he would turn the Soviet Union into one giant factory, so one of Coase's unanswered questions at the time was whether there was any natural limit to how big a company could be and whether you actually needed companies at all.

The prevailing economic theory of the time, based on the work of Adam Smith, was that because markets were efficient, it should always be cheaper to contract out than to hire. By the time Coase returned from the United States, he had started to form a very different view. He wrote a short, but highly influential paper called "The Nature of the Firm" (1937), in which he argued that companies exist to lower the transaction costs incurred should you need to use the market every time you need to get something done.

He predicted the rise of companies that could produce internally all the components and systems they need to create their end-product, rather than spending money on what we would consider outsourcing (e.g., recruiting via agents). In his opinion, anything that had to be done could be done more cheaply in-house than by hiring someone from outside. Sixty years later, that paper would earn him a Nobel Prize in economics.

But if firms only exist to either reduce or eliminate transaction costs, what if technology like blockchain could do this more effectively? Would the firm as a concept still need to exist in its current form?

Leaving aside the speculative nature of cryptocurrencies like Bitcoin, blockchain is a profound idea that will likely change the structure of companies in the twenty-first century. Blockchains work like giant distributed databases, allowing buyers and sellers to store and exchange value, and validating transactions without using intermediaries.

Ethereum, for example, is a platform that runs its own blockchain and has a protocol that allows for smart contracts. Smart contracts are agreements written in code; you could write one that governs a rental agreement for a house or specifies the royalties for a song or a movie, for example. Gaurang Torvekar, co-founder and CTO of smart contracts startup Attores, and his fiancée, Sayalee Kaluskar, even decided to use a smart contract to create a prenuptial agreement that specified, among other things, how much of the couple's time should be spent watching *The Walking Dead* relative to episodes of *Seinfeld*.

In the future, some firms may operate without people or locations. They will be "decentralized autonomous organizations" based entirely on smart contracts that react to data and other algorithms. Even if you don't subscribe to such a radical vision of tomorrow's firm, there may be parts of your organization—perhaps even entire departments—that have the potential to be automated or decentralized.

My advice? If you think there is chance that algorithms could transform your part of the business, it is always better to lead the charge rather than wait for marching orders.

SUMMARY

1 The algorithmic age is a "winner-takes-all" era: the leaders who think big and invest in scale will be in the best position for continued success. Don't fall into the trap of letting your *digital transformation* become *digital incrementalism*.

2 Great ideas from the past can hold you back from exploring new opportunities. Design your organization to be agile enough to look beyond past successes to embrace new capabilities without being slowed by rigid structures, hierarchies, and workflows.

3 True algorithmic innovation demands more than just serious computation and financial investment; it requires interesting data.

Algorithms are only as good as the data you train them on. Let finding and developing compelling data be a core driver of your strategic plans.

4 Large organizations have an advantage when it comes to data if they are willing to leverage it. To do so requires assembling the right teams and partners and systematically identifying the parts of your business with the greatest potential for algorithmic reinvention.

5 Algorithmic technologies like the blockchain and smart contracts challenge the traditional structure of firms and raise the question of whether parts of them will even exist in the future. The future of your company may be no company at all.

QUESTION

What is something that your organization does today that might run autonomously on blockchain in the future?

THINK
COMPUTATIONALLY

*"Machine learning is a core, transformative way
by which we're rethinking how we're doing everything."*
SUNDAR PICHAI, CEO OF GOOGLE

Start with first principles

Computational thinking is an approach to solving problems and making decisions that allows you to leverage data and technology to augment your capabilities. Although the concept was popularized by Jeannette Wing, former head of computer science at Carnegie Mellon, it is really just a form of "first principles thinking," a technique that has been around since the time of Aristotle.

Wing has explained computational thinking as "the thought processes involved in formulating problems and their solutions so that the solutions are represented in a form that can effectively be carried out by an information-processing agent." That is a complex way of saying that computational thinking is a structured approach to problem solving, which ultimately allows you to come up with a solution that can be effectively carried out by computers, people, or—typically—a combination of both.

A good starting point if you want to learn how to be a more effective computational thinker is to understand the difference between reasoning by analogy and reasoning from first principles.

Analogies are a particular type of inductive argument in which perceived similarities are used to imply some further similarity. They can be a powerful way to teach a lesson because they engage the narrative, story-driven part of our brain. But that also means they are potentially limiting, as the perceived similarity between two situations can hide more fundamental truths, which when thoroughly explored might lead you to radically different conclusions.

One of the things that fascinated me as a law student was how much of the legal world was governed by such stories, many of which were strange and obscure. Take the infamous case of someone drinking a bottle of ginger beer that contained a dead snail in the Scottish town of Paisley, Renfrewshire, in 1928. Even today, that case, *Donoghue v. Stevenson*, influences our thinking about product liability and how we should handle problems like exploding

Samsung smartphones. When lawyers reason by analogy, they will generally try to persuade a judge that a case whose facts may be materially different is nevertheless governed by the same general principles as the situation at hand. This allows them to demonstrate that there is a legal precedent that supports their argument and that a decision in their favor would be part of a long line of judicial thinking on the matter.

It is not only lawyers who use analogies to persuade. If you happen to meet a famous Hollywood studio executive in an elevator, you may have only moments to pitch your movie script that has been sitting in your bottom drawer for years. To save time, you might use an analogy based on other movies they might be familiar with. Perhaps your idea is to make *The Matrix* meets *The Notebook*, in the historical setting of *Gladiator*. Should that be the case, I can only hope for all our sakes that yours will be a very short elevator ride.

Algorithmic leaders take a different approach to evaluating problems and making decisions. They tend to approach strategic issues in a more structured way that allows them to use data and computation to augment their problem-solving capabilities. That's where a traditional Hollywood studio executive might differ from someone who works on the content production team at Netflix. Analogies are not enough, and they can be misleading if you don't have the data to support the purported similarities. As simple as that sounds, it goes against much of twentieth-century management training, which traditionally coached leaders to reason by analogy rather than first principles.

Management students analyze business cases and prepare arguments based on what other companies or leaders have done in similar situations. For example, fans of Harvard Business School professor Clayton Christensen take case studies, like the rise of minimills in the 1970s, which disrupted the steel business, as proof of larger strategic trends. Minimills initially made cheap concrete-reinforcing bars known as rebar. Larger competitors, like U.S. Steel, were not fazed by this development—until the minimills used their success to navigate their way into the production of higher-value products.

Intel's CEO at the time, Andy Grove, interpreted the minimill analogy as a warning to not cede the bottom of the market, and so he started promoting Intel's low-end Celeron processor more aggressively to buyers of cheaper computers. But the analogy failed Grove and Intel in an important way: they completely missed the rise of the smartphone market. Intel's real threat was in fact ARM, a tiny British chip design company with a market cap that, for most of the pre-iPhone era, was smaller than Intel's marketing budget. When Steve Jobs asked Intel if they wanted to fabricate a chip based on a design licensed from ARM for his new iPhone, Intel refused. It didn't want to be in the low-margin business of providing phone CPUs, and it simply didn't realize just how big the smartphone revolution would be.

Reasoning by analogy alone not only is dangerous when it comes to strategy, but also can create confusion when it comes to culture and leadership. All too often we try to teach leaders concepts like team building by making them take part in a tug-of-war or a "trust-fall" (a trust-building game in which a person deliberately allows themselves to fall, relying on someone else to catch them).

Don't get me wrong. Whether it be paintball or making houses with playing cards, company social activities can be fun and an excellent opportunity to interact and get to know each other. But do these activities, built on analogous thinking as they are, also reinforce a way of thinking that is counterproductive?

If you are trying to secure support for a breakthrough product, how can you obtain funding when your superiors demand examples of similar successful products in the market? When a marketing team develops a campaign that replicates the approach of the number one player in the market, is this good work or poor judgment?

When your engineering team tells you that the brilliant design for a new device can't be built at a reasonable cost, do you merely accept what they say? That last question is particularly relevant, as it is part of the Space Exploration Technologies (SpaceX) story.

When Elon Musk set out to acquire his first rockets with a view to taking people to Mars one day, he faced a seemingly insurmountable problem: cost. The cheapest US rockets that could do the job cost $65 million each, and he would need two. He therefore went to Russia to find out whether he could buy some repurposed intercontinental ballistic missiles that the Russians were apparently selling to any interested buyer. Even without nuclear warheads attached, the price of the Russian rockets was between $15 million and $20 million each. So how did Musk, six years after starting SpaceX, manage to put his first rocket, *Falcon 1*, into orbit at a price to his customers—*not his cost*—of $7 million?

Musk used first principles thinking. Aristotle defined a *first principle* as "the first basis from which a thing is known." First principles thinking is therefore the art of breaking a problem down to the fundamental parts that you know are true and building up from there.

As he flew back from his meeting with the Russians, Musk started to wonder what a rocket was actually made of. If you were to break a rocket down into all its constituent pieces, how much would those cost?

After some research, he discovered rockets were principally composed of aerospace-grade aluminum alloys, plus some titanium, copper, and carbon fiber. When he investigated the value of those materials on the commodities market, he realized that the actual cost of materials was only around 2 per cent of the typical price of a rocket. Musk decided that by assembling the right team and applying the latest technology in design and manufacturing, he could make a much cheaper rocket from scratch. That was the beginning of not only SpaceX but also a new era in commercial spaceflight.

This is not the only example of Musk's using first principles thinking. When he was advised that it was impossible to cost-effectively use batteries to store energy for homes and cars, he once again broke the problem down into smaller parts. He reasoned that the material constituents of batteries might differ from their assembled cost. If you were to buy carbon, nickel, aluminum, polymers, and a steel housing on a metals exchange, what would that cost? Much less, it turned out, than people assumed.

To successfully reason from first principles, you first need to identify your current assumptions and then break them down into their fundamental truths before exploring how you might create new solutions from scratch.

Now that you understand the basic approach of first principles thinking, it is time to use it in a way that will allow you to work more effectively with algorithms and AI. Knowing how to program a computer is not as important as knowing how to think in a way that allows computers to help you be more effective. Rather than *artificial intelligence*, think of it as *augmented intelligence*.

So, how does the algorithmic age change the way that you, as a business leader, approach making important decisions and solving difficult problems? Let's find out.

Think like a computer

Like reasoning from first principles, computational thinking involves taking a problem and breaking it down into a series of smaller, more manageable problems (decomposition). These problems can then be considered in the context of how similar problems might have been tackled in the past (pattern recognition). Next, you can identify simple steps or rules to solve each of the smaller problems (algorithms), before considering what the bigger picture might be (abstraction).

You can express these principles as a series of steps, applicable to any problem:

1 Break a problem into parts or steps
2 Recognize and find patterns or trends
3 Develop instructions to solve a problem or steps for a task
4 Generalize patterns and trends into rules, principles, or insights

What makes computational thinking, as opposed to mathematical or theoretical thinking, useful in the real world is that it incorporates practical constraints. When facing a particular challenge, an algorithmic leader might consider how difficult a problem is to solve, the best way to solve it, how long the available computing resources might take to do it, and whether an approximate solution might be good enough. From this perspective, computational thinking is about reformulating seemingly intractable problems into ones that we know how to solve by reducing or transforming them in some way.

You might use computational thinking to work out where your best employees come from, to determine the real reason your customers don't renew their contracts, why there are constant breakdowns on your production line, or even which of your marketing strategies is actually working. Computational thinking is simply a structured, iterative approach that takes into account all the data now available for us to hone our judgment calls.

However, aside from making you a smarter leader, computational thinking has the potential to change the way we do things at a bigger scale, and in doing so, transform entire professions. For example, consider the way that semiconductor chips are tested.

Chips are routinely tested at the manufacturing stage, which is also when they are embedded into a device such as a phone or a tablet. Typically this would be a job performed by a test engineer using specialist equipment. It is time-consuming, expensive, and increasingly complex as our devices get smaller and more sophisticated. But what if there were a better way?

Keith Schaub, who is a VP at Advantest, a company that makes chip-testing equipment, explained to me the value of computational thinking in his field, using the analogy of baseball.

He told me to imagine two coaches, each with the job of selecting the best possible team. One coach does what most good coaches do: he devises a series of tests and challenges to work out whether a player has the requisite ability and skill. A potential player either passes or fails this process, in the same way that a chip might pass or fail when tested. It takes a long time to run these tests, because every single player has to be individually assessed.

The other coach, who is a natural computational thinker, decides not to test everyone. She instead goes through the school and medical records of all the players. She looks through the data on how well they played in the past, their physical attributes, and how they have been trained. Using a simple machine learning model that correlates this data with previously successful players in past years, she is able to come up with almost the same list as the other coach—without testing everyone. This, in essence, is how Schaub sees the future of chip testing. There is a lot of available data that test engineers have previously collected about the reliability and performance of chips, particularly in combination with certain kinds of wafers (the semiconductor material that chips are made from). Their real job in the future will not be testing chips, but rather working with AI and machine learning platforms to devise smarter ways of predicting failure, and refining these models with time.

Augment your intelligence

One of the main advantages of computational thinking is that it offers the ability to separate the strategy (how to approach a problem) from the execution (crunching the data). When you get the combination right, you can tackle problems of a completely differ-ent order—like finding exoplanets, for example.

An exoplanet is a planet that orbits a star outside our solar sys-tem. The Kepler telescope was launched by NASA on March 7, 2009, with the mission of finding such Earth-sized planets orbit-ing other stars. It works by detecting the shadows planets cast as they orbit their parent stars. When a planet passes in front of its star, the Kepler telescope detects a minuscule dimming of the light.

Kepler has observed 150,000 such stars to date and already dis-covered more than 4,000 candidate planets, of which about 2,300 have been confirmed. Automated tests, and sometimes human eyes, were used to verify signals in the data that seemed the most prom-ising. But given the vast amounts of data involved and the weakness of some signals, some astronomers wondered if they had missed anything.

Christopher Shallue, a senior software engineer at Google, was curious about whether there might be some new and interest-ing applications of machine learning and, in particular, situations where there was so much data that humans might not be able to search it effectively themselves. He became interested in exoplanet discovery after learning that astronomy, like other branches of sci-ence, was rapidly being inundated with data, typically faster than our ability to manually examine it.

So, in his spare time, he started googling "finding exoplanets with large datasets," which brought him to the Kepler mission and the vast dataset it had generated. He got in touch with Andrew Van-derburg, an astronomer at the University of Texas at Austin.

After discussing the problem, the pair came up with the idea of training a neural network to identify examples of when a planet was passing in front of its star, using a training dataset of signals from the Kepler catalog of exoplanets that had already been confirmed. Once the neural network was able to correctly identify true planets and avoid false positives 96 per cent of the time, they set it to work looking for weaker signals across 670 star systems that already had multiple known planets, hoping that perhaps something interesting had been missed. That's when they discovered Kepler-90i.

Like Earth, Kepler-90i is the third rock from its sun, although it is considerably hotter than our home planet. The eight planets in the Kepler-90 system are scrunched into the equivalent distance of Earth to the sun with extremely tight orbits. A year on Kepler-90i lasts only 14.4 days. This was the first time a star system with as many planets as our own solar system had been discovered way out in deep space.

Finding a time to talk with Vanderburg wasn't easy. When I contacted him, he was in the midst of astronomical observations that required him to stay awake most nights—not an easy routine to maintain, even for someone passionate about looking at stars. I asked him what attracted him to this field. When he finished college, he said, he looked at the physics students. And then he looked at the astronomy students. The astronomers, he said, seemed to be a lot happier on average than the physicists.

Although people often focus on how humans and AI can work together effectively, what fascinated me about the story of Vanderburg and Shallue's partnership was that it was a case of machine learning bringing together two *human* professionals from very different fields.

"When we first met, we decided to focus on a problem that astronomers were struggling to find an answer to, as opposed to finding a problem that astronomers kind of already have a good handle on that we could maybe replicate with new computational techniques," explained Vanderburg. "The problem we chose was measuring how common it was for water to exist in liquid form on the surface in our galaxy. This was the whole point of Kepler, to measure this quantity, this frequency. People have made attempts over the years, and there have been lots of papers trying to measure it. But fundamentally, the challenge has been that Kepler just wasn't quite sensitive enough to do it. So our goal at first was to try to see if we can move along this path. And I think that's helped us, because instead of trying to do something totally new, we tried to do something where there was already quite a lot of progress made, which made it easier for us to hit the ground running."

For Vanderburg, the partnership worked because both he and Shallue brought something very different to the equation. Vanderburg had deep domain expertise and a knowledge of both where the field of astronomy was going and the exciting problems worth focusing on. He also had practical knowledge relevant to the project, such as knowing how to open, manipulate, and interpret the Kepler data.

Shallue was an expert in convolutional neural networks, image classification, image captioning, and the dynamics of deep networks. He had an intuition for what would work and what wouldn't when you build those kinds of networks, which saved a lot of time and wandering down wrong paths.

As you contemplate forming AI projects in your organization, Vanderburg and Shallue's story is a good one to remember. A good AI team requires more than just a collection of AI experts; it requires a practical diversity of skills, knowledge, and perspectives.

Computational thinking and the use of AI will transform many fields of research in coming years, from drug R&D to anthropology to architecture. For example, in the area of materials science, scientists will be able to tell an AI what they want to create—say, a superstrong material—and the AI will tell the scientists the best experiment to run to create it.

The discovery of Kepler-90 was more than simply the discovery of a new star system; it was also a demonstration of how in the future we will be using algorithms rather than the naked eye to scan the skies. Soon, we will explore the frontiers of the cosmos through data, with machines and algorithms tasked with the heavy lifting.

Computers still need us to solve complex problems. The real skill in a world where computational platforms can assist with the search process is being able to correctly and creatively dissect and frame a problem to help the computer begin to solve it.

Learn to trust the algorithm

Preparing yourself and your teams to think and approach problems in a way that computers can help you is an important step, but how prepared are you to trust algorithms to make decisions for you? Learning to trust algorithmic systems is not easy for most people; in fact, distrust of automated systems is an issue that dates back to when people first started offloading work to machines.

In the early days of NASA's space program, as described by Tom Wolfe in *The Right Stuff*, those chosen to ride in the largely automated Mercury space capsules were test pilots, people who, after a high-adrenaline career of life-or-death decisions, didn't particularly like the idea of riding in a metal can without any manual controls. In fact, test pilot Al Shephard, the first American in space, did so little during his first fifteen-minute flight that his co-pilots later ridiculed him by calling him "spam in a can." In Wolfe's view, radar operators might have been better suited to the task, given the passive observation required for the job.

The test pilots lobbied hard and were eventually granted manual overrides, altitude controls, and emergency hatches. Unfortunately, their aversion to automation and their ability to make their own decisions in life-or-death situations also led to errors that, ironically, almost cost them their lives. Test pilots are not alone. Although in many fields and applications algorithms consistently outperform humans, people often fail to use them, a phenomenon known as *algorithm aversion.*

The idea of algorithm aversion is a theme that Jason Collins, who runs the data science team at ASIC, the Australian financial regulator, has explored in his research into behavioral science. In his view, despite stories about freestyle chess and the effectiveness of human-machine combinations, there is growing evidence that for some types of decisions, a person + algorithm situation results in worse outcomes than an algorithm working alone. A major factor in these poor outcomes is that even if the algorithm suggests the correct course of action, humans simply refuse to follow the computer's advice.

For Collins, one of the best ways in which organizations can help their leaders overcome their algorithm aversion of decisions better left to machines is by benchmarking. By tracking the results of your cognitive systems and comparing them against people who are making decisions in a wide variety of areas, you can both get a sense of where humans excel relative to machines and help other leaders see where they should be focusing their time.

While benchmarking algorithmic performance against the performance of experts in your company is one way of building trust, another approach is simply to compromise and provide a little bit of control, even if it leads to suboptimal results. This is essentially what NASA chose to do when it allowed its test pilots to have manual overrides. An interesting example of this from the academic world is a piece of research conducted by Berkeley Dietvorst, Joseph Simmons, and Cade Massey. They ran an experiment in which they gave participants the ability to modify the impact of an algorithm. They discovered that this increased the likelihood that it would actually be used, even if participants would have been better off by not interfering at all.

One way of overcoming algorithm aversion, without compromising the effectiveness of a system, is to allow the humans who need to trust the algorithm to be personally involved in designing safety controls and operating boundaries.

In 2016, DeepMind worked with Google to develop an AI-powered recommendation system to improve the energy efficiency of Google's data centers, where its search platform and services like YouTube and Gmail are powered. A data center is a highly dynamic environment, which makes thermal management a complex challenge and inherently problematic in terms of applying simple rules for management. The equipment, how the engineers operate that equipment, and the environment interact with each other in complex, nonlinear ways. Throw in weather changes and the fact that each data center has a unique physical architecture and environmental conditions, and you have a serious operating challenge. However, by using machine learning, DeepMind was able to generate specific recommendations for human operators to implement in real time that ended up reducing the amount of energy Google used for cooling by up to 40 per cent.

While an impressive result, the DeepMind algorithm was not at that stage in direct control of the cooling system. That took two more years. The challenge was not the technology, but coming up with an AI safety regime that allowed Google's leaders to trust the machine with full autonomy.

Now, every five minutes, a cloud-based AI analyzes the data center cooling system from thousands of sensors and feeds the data into deep neural networks that predict how different combinations of potential actions will affect future energy consumption. The algorithm then identifies which actions will minimize energy consumption while satisfying a set of safety constraints, before automatically communicating with the data center, where the actions are verified by a local control system before being implemented.

This last stage of verification is where human engineers play a key role. Google calls it two-layer verification. The optimal actions recommended by the AI are checked against an internal list of safety constraints defined by their data center operators. This check ensures that even though the AI system has direct control, it remains within local constraints and operators retain full control of the operating boundaries.

As I was exploring the idea of algorithm aversion, I kept returning to the story of the space program and the puzzle of whether to grant autonomy to sophisticated systems that didn't need much intervention or trust capable human beings who were trained to execute excellent interventions. So when I got a chance to speak to Scott Kelly, the first American to spend almost a full year (it was 340 consecutive days, so close enough) in space, I couldn't resist asking him about his views on the subject.

For Kelly, technology and automated systems had always played a central role during his experiences in space. On his first flight, on New Year's Eve in 1999, NASA ended the mission early so that the shuttle could land before 2000 rolled over. They were concerned about Y2K making their systems go haywire.

"I think they were worried," he said with a wry smile, "that the space shuttle would shut down or enter a wormhole or something."

On the subject of manual controls, Kelly explained that NASA was discussing this all the time with Jeff Bezos and Elon Musk. The new generation of space barons tend to favor as much automation as possible, with little input from humans. NASA would prefer to give astronauts whatever they need to maximize their chance of survival.

Kelly tended to agree with NASA's viewpoint, although he said that AI was changing things. From his personal experience, it used to be the case that the auto-lander on the space shuttle couldn't do as good a job as a human at the controls, but that was changing rapidly. And, he added, it may come down to cost. Would it really be worth spending an extra billion dollars for a few controls that may or may not increase the chance of survival for the crew? In an age of commercial space flight, rather than government space programs, the answer may well be no.

Speak the languages of power

The final step in your journey to becoming a true computational thinker is to be able to express your ideas and test your strategies in specialist, domain-specific languages.

Being able to use a domain-specific language is not quite the same as being able to program in a language like Python or JavaScript, as it requires an understanding of both coding and business. This is because, unlike a normal programming language, domain-specific commands are not used to build software applications but to express business transactions, ideas, or strategies in formal, structured logic. Not surprisingly, one of the first areas in which we are likely to see algorithmic leaders using such languages are activities already transformed by algorithmic models, such as investment and trading.

As I was researching how algorithms were changing the finance industry, I came across Manoj Narang. A proponent of high-frequency trading (HFT), he previously founded Tradeworx before setting up electronic trading and asset manager Mana Partners, with $1 billion in funds under management. Although there is a growing number of algorithmic hedge funds, many larger than Mana, what makes Narang interesting is his unique vision for the investment manager of the future: a supersmart human augmented by even smarter AI.

In Narang's view, there are many industries, his own included, where you might imagine that a small group of people should be able to run a complex business without having hundreds of programmers on staff. That only becomes possible if your programmers have built the right infrastructure and high-level languages that then allow business people to execute their ideas, design processes, and build powerful applications.

Typically in an investment firm, ideas are created by one set of people with financial skills and implemented by an entirely different set of people who know nothing about investments or markets. At his own firm, Narang sought to circumvent that by vertically integrating the company's technology and creating domain-specific languages that allow strategists to do everything.

You can think of a domain-specific language as one that exposes the most important, primitive elements of a business in a highly expressive way as part of the semantics of the language. That matters, because a general programming language is more focused on issues like data structures, memory management, and other abstract concepts that have little to do with the business in question.

In Narang's view, the most highly compensated and coveted people in the future won't necessarily be the most skilled programmers or the smartest MBA graduates. They will be the people who can live at the intersection of technology and business, who can devise and drive the domain-specific languages that will allow them to shape and reshape their business model.

Whether it be optimizing a global supply chain, crafting a data-driven marketing campaign, or coordinating a freelance workforce, some of the most effective leaders of the future will not only need to think computationally, they will also have to be able to express their ideas directly in algorithmic language.

SUMMARY

1 If you want to improve the way you think, start by understanding the difference between reasoning by analogy and reasoning from first principles. Reasoning by analogy leads you to compare like with like—a limiting prospect. Using first principles allows you to take a problem apart and look at it again from the perspective of its fundamental truths.

2 Like reasoning from first principles, computational thinking is a structured approach to problem solving that allows you to leverage data and algorithms to be more effective. When you think in this way, AI and machine learning platforms can help you devise smarter ways of predicting outcomes and generating insights.

3 The story of how Christopher Shallue and Andrew Vanderburg used machine learning to discover a new exoplanet illustrates

not only the potential of computational astronomy and other new algorithmic approaches to research, but also the importance of team design when it comes to best leveraging AI for solving problems.

4 A key barrier to computational thinking in your organization is algorithm aversion, or human mistrust of the recommendations made by an AI system. Sometimes the best way to get people to trust algorithms is to involve them in the design and management of an algorithmic safety process.

5 In the future, the most effective computational thinkers will be those who can directly express their ideas and execute their strategies in domain-specific programming languages.

QUESTION

If you were to reimagine your traditional business activities—for example, marketing, sales, finance, and logistics—as computational marketing, computational sales, computational finance, or computational logistics, how would they need to change?

EMBRACE UNCERTAINTY

"Without gambling, I would not exist."
HUNTER S. THOMPSON

See the world like a gambler

One of the unfortunate side effects of living in an age of accelerating technology is having to deal with increased uncertainty. When faced with uncertainty, how should leaders react? Should they make a big bet, hedge their position, or just wait and see?

We tend to see situations in one of two ways: either events are certain and can therefore be managed by planning, investment, and reliable budgets; or they are uncertain, and we cannot manage them.

You can, however, embrace uncertainty by adjusting your views as new information becomes available. In order to do that, you need to learn something about Thomas Bayes, an English clergyman and mathematician who proposed a theorem in 1763 that would forever change the way we think about making decisions in ambiguous conditions.

Bayes was interested in how our beliefs about the world should evolve as we accumulate new but unproven evidence. Specifically, he wondered how he could predict the probability of a future event if he only knew how many times it had occurred, or not, in the past. To answer that, he constructed a thought experiment.

Imagine a billiard table. You put on a blindfold and your assistant randomly rolls a ball across the table. They take note of where it stops rolling. Your job is to figure out where the ball is. All you can really do at this point is make a random guess.

Now imagine that you ask your assistant to drop some more balls on the table and tell you whether they stop to the left or right of the first ball. If all the balls stop to the right, what can you say about the position of the first ball? If more balls are thrown, how does this improve your knowledge of the position of the first ball? In fact, throw after throw, you should be able to narrow down the area in which the first ball probably lies. Bayes figured out that even when it comes to uncertain outcomes, we can update our knowledge by incorporating new, relevant information as it becomes available.

Many years later, French mathematician Pierre-Simon Laplace developed Bayes's idea into a powerful theory, which we now know as the Bayes Theorem. Here is a simple explanation of it.

Beginning with a provisional hypothesis about the world, assign to it an initial probability of that event happening, called the prior probability or simply the prior. After collecting new, relevant evidence, recalculate the probability of the hypothesis in light of the new evidence. This revised probability is called the posterior probability.

You can find evidence of Bayesian thinking throughout modern history, from nineteenth-century French and Russian artillery officers adjusting their cannons to Alan Turing trying to crack the German Enigma codes. Bayes has even influenced the design of machine learning techniques, notably the naive Bayes classifier.

Bayes is relevant to modern leaders because it can help them develop an approach to uncertainty that is less deterministic and more probabilistic. Even when events are determined by an infinitely complex set of factors, probabilistic thinking can help you identify the likeliest outcomes and so make the best decisions. Viewing the information probabilistically enables you to describe one of many possible outcomes, some more or less likely than others.

One of the key advantages of thinking probabilistically is that it equips you with a more critical perspective to evaluate new data as it becomes available. Data can be imperfect, incomplete, or uncertain. There is often more than one explanation for why things happened the way they did; by examining those alternative explanations using probability, you can gain a better understanding of causality and what is really going on.

Deterministic models produce a single solution that describes the outcome of an experiment given appropriate inputs; in other words, for every possible input, there is a single output. A probabilistic model distributes over all possible solutions and provides some indication of how likely it is that each will, might, or can occur.

The human mind is naturally deterministic. We generally believe that something is true or false. Either you like someone or you don't. There is rarely a situation when you can say that there is a 46 per cent probability that someone is your friend. In fact, unless you are a teenager and have a lot of frenemies, you are probably quite deterministic about your social circle. Our instinct for determinism may well have been an evolutionary innovation. To survive, we had to make snap judgments about the world and our response to it. When a tiger is approaching you, there is really not a lot of time to consider whether he's approaching as a friend or a foe.

However, the deterministic approach that kept our ancestors alive while hunting in the savannah won't help you make good decisions in complex, unpredictable environments when your natural mental shortcuts and heuristics start to fail you. One of the best ways to embrace uncertainty and be more probabilistic in your approach is to learn to think like a professional gambler. Take, for example, Rasmus Ankersen.

Ankersen, a Dane living in London, originally came to the UK to look for an English publisher for his book on human performance, the writing of which had taken him from Kenya to Korea in search of why great athletes, whether they are runners or golfers, tend to come from the same small regions. One of the reasons he decided to stay in London was a chance meeting with a professional gambler named Matthew Benham.

Benham is a renowned, albeit somewhat inaccessible, figure in the British gambling world. After graduating from the University of Oxford with a physics degree, he went into securities trading, first at Yamaichi International and then at the Bank of America. This was followed by a stint working as a trader for Premier Bet with Tony Bloom, one of the most successful gamblers in the world. That inspired Benham to leave his day job and focus on gambling. He went on to start two successful gaming companies, Matchbook, a sports betting exchange community, and Smartodds, which provides statistical research and sports modeling services.

When Ankersen and Benham met, they started talking about how soccer (except, of course, they called it football) was a sport that was yet to be disrupted by data and probabilistic thinking. Benham was impressed enough to invite Ankersen to help run Brentford Football Club, which he had recently acquired. Soon after, Benham also bought Midtjylland, the soccer club in Ankersen's hometown.

Ankersen's insight was this: soccer is one of the world's unfairest sports. Although there is a saying that "the league table never lies," in Ankersen's opinion that is exactly what it does. Because soccer is a low-scoring sport, the win/loss outcome of a game is not an accurate representation of the actual performance of a team, and therefore the intrinsic value of its players. From a professional gambler's perspective, the key to placing a good bet is to continually update your position with relevant insights that impact the probability of an event occurring. Rather than trying to be right, gamblers try to be less wrong with time.

Benham and Ankersen started to use the scientific application of statistics—the "moneyball" technique pioneered in baseball—when assessing the performance of a team. Their key performance metric became "expected goals" for and against a team, based on the quality and quantity of chances created during a match. The point of this exercise was to develop an alternative league table, which might serve as a more reliable predictor of results and a better basis on which to value and acquire players.

As an algorithmic leader, you will also find having a probabilistic mindset useful, and not just when you want to place a bet in the office fantasy soccer competition. Let's consider a few examples.

A probabilistic HR manager will examine the data about where a company's best people come from and how they perform throughout their career to identify new sources of talent that may have been overlooked.

A probabilistic sales professional will be conscious that it's not enough to simply close lots of deals; it's important to also think about where leads come from. How many opportunities were created organically, as opposed to being fed through an existing pipeline? How many new customers churn after just a few months? By understanding the data around which leads go on to become great customers, a sales leader can then work closely with their marketing colleagues to figure out new sources of potential customer prospects.

Probabilistic risk managers will think about the future of how they work. While their job may have been setting or applying strict credit policies in the past, they may now start to wonder whether their traditional credit rating models are still effective. Are there low-risk segments in their customer base that they may have missed and that a new competitor may be able to target?

Developing a probabilistic mindset allows you to be better prepared for the uncertainties and complexities of the algorithmic age. Even when events are determined by an infinitely complex set of factors, probabilistic thinking can help us identify the most likely outcomes and the best decisions to make.

Rethink the role of meetings

Unless you work alone, the reality of modern organizations is that decision making involves other people and stakeholders. To effectively embrace uncertainty, you have to also consider the ways in which groups of people process information and reach conclusions. For the most part, that means thinking hard about meetings and how to make them better.

The culture of meetings is entrenched in modern organizations. They are so prevalent that we rarely question their purpose or existence—even in the midst of a radical transformation, when everything else, every other process, is up for review, the meeting culture survives. And algorithmic organizations are no different. In fact, as you automate more decisions and processes, the quality time that humans spend together on strategic and complex issues becomes even more critical.

Meetings can be powerful forums for solving problems and securing support for projects. They are also a reflection of your work culture. From that perspective, there is no single right way to run a good meeting, just as there is no culture that works for everyone. That said, there are some "hacks" that can help you focus your meeting so you make high-quality decisions rather than waste time.

Perhaps the simplest way to improve a meeting is to keep it brief. Personal discomfort is a classic technique for ensuring brevity. Whenever the Privy Council of the United Kingdom meets, all the participants have to stand. Legend has it that this practice was initiated by Queen Victoria following the death of Albert, Prince Consort, when she wished to keep her public duties to the absolute minimum. Without chairs to recline in, her advisers tended to keep things succinct.

It is funny to think that Queen Victoria may have also inspired the creators of the Agile software movement. Agile developers have a daily fifteen-minute meeting (which they call a scrum meeting) for product development teams, during which time everyone has to stand up—this keeps things on track. Much of the Agile approach to software development is about managing uncertainty. Developers accept that they don't know everything they might need to know about a project before they start, so the process and the use of meetings are designed to adapt both the solution and the process as the project progresses.

Some companies, like the online shoe retailer Zappos, have taken an extreme approach to redesigning meetings by adopting formal protocols for communication that resemble a kind of computer program. The similarity to software is probably no accident, since Zappos has embraced Holacracy, a radical system of organizational design created by Brian Robertson, a former programmer.

At Zappos, there are no job titles, only roles, and people in the organization can hold multiple roles at any given time. In

Holacratic companies, a role is a series of accountabilities and activities that are defined by circles (or teams) and managed by a formal governance process. Ironically, all of this non-hierarchical, self-organization requires that when circles meet at Zappos, they have to communicate in a very structured, technical, and highly organized way.

Holacracy is not for everyone. Watching a circle meet is quite weird, actually; it can seem more like people playing Dungeons & Dragons than getting things done. It also shows, though, that there is a science behind how information is gathered, processed, and decided upon in a meeting. The more you can understand about the meeting mechanics that drive good outcomes in your own culture, the more consistent results you will achieve.

The science of good meetings was something that obsessed Andy Grove, former CEO of Intel. He believed that meetings were such an essential part of Intel's culture that for many years he taught a class on meeting basics for new employees. If you walked into any meeting room, or even a factory, at Intel during that time, you would see a poster on the wall with a series of questions about the meetings that took place there: Do you know the purpose of this meeting? Do you have an agenda? Do you know your role? Do you follow the rules for good minutes?

For every meeting, Intel had a formal agenda template. This agenda, circulated before each meeting, listed the key topics, who would lead which parts of the discussion, how long they would take, and the expected outcomes. They also specified the meeting's decision-making style, which helped set the attendees' expectations up front. At Intel, a decision was said to reflect one of four styles: authoritative (the leader has full responsibility); consultative (the leader makes a decision after weighing group input); voting; or consensus.

Amazon also has a unique way of running meetings. For starters, they have banned slide decks. If you want to get a decision made, you need to bring a memo, no more than six pages long, structured in a logical way, with supporting data in the appendices. Every meeting at Amazon generally begins with fifteen minutes of silent reading time, followed by the attendees making high-level comments about an idea before going through the memo page by page, providing feedback.

Data-driven meetings at Amazon work because teams at Amazon are also generally small. How small? Jeff Bezos is famous for having said that a team should never be so big that it couldn't be fed by two pizzas. I wasn't sure how big that was, so when I had the opportunity to visit Amazon's headquarters in Seattle, I asked someone. Turns out that a two-pizza team at Amazon means somewhere between three and eight people. Bezos's rationale for keeping things small is that once you have big teams, people waste time on chasing consensus rather than focusing on creating disruptive ideas.

Once a project is approved at Amazon, a "single threaded owner" is assigned to it to make sure that one person is totally focused on the customer delivery. More than anything else, Amazon values speed and agility, rather than collaboration and consensus. In fact, there can often be multiple small teams working on the same issue— almost competitively—to see who can solve the problem first.

Understanding the science of your own meetings and developing structures, templates, and frameworks are important steps in ensuring that your teams are gathering all the relevant data, adjusting their approaches, and making high-quality decisions. Good meetings are an essential weapon as you wage war against uncertainty.

Be aware, however, that there is also danger in overengineering meetings. If you start dictating the way people should communicate, present ideas, or make decisions, you may run the risk of stifling rather than stimulating human creativity.

Not only is it worth thinking about the form and structure of meetings, it's also important to pay attention to their purpose and values. Bad meetings are a symptom, rather than the cause of ineffective organizations. If you have adopted a culture of transparency, where data and facts drive decisions, projects are coordinated by algorithms, and work is done by small, empowered teams, the primary function of meetings becomes problem solving and creative development, rather than compliance and control.

Interestingly, the performance of teams in solving problems and developing new ideas may have less to do with who is part of them and more to do with their shared values.

Google spent two years studying 180 of its teams. It called the study Project Aristotle. The researchers discovered that the best teams at Google exhibit a range of soft skills or "group norms": equality, generosity, curiosity about teammates' ideas, empathy, and emotional intelligence. The study's most famous finding was that the most significant attribute of a successful team was not the number of geniuses in it, but the degree of emotional safety. That is, the degree to which people felt safe to propose new ideas, take risks, share divergent opinions, and ask judgment-free questions determined how successful their teams were in executing their projects. Google found that teams with psychologically safe environments had employees who were less likely to leave, generated more diverse ideas, and ultimately made more impact. That's the one consolation of uncertainty: you are not the only one facing it.

Conduct a decision audit

Making decisions in uncertain conditions is difficult. Even more difficult is deciding which decisions are worth making.

Some decisions are "make or break." Get them right, and they will fast-track your career or company. Get them wrong, and they will condemn you to an eternity of trying to fix your mistake, or worse, wondering "what if?" So how do you figure out which decisions are so important that they deserve to take up your time? You need to conduct a decision audit. This means thinking strategically about the kinds of decisions that matter, and then ensuring there is a mechanism for them to be made quickly and well by the people on your team.

Most algorithmic organizations have faced decisive moments that demanded the strategic judgment of humans, rather than machines. Netflix, having built a successful business based on sending out DVDs in red envelopes, had to decide whether to continue distributing content in that way or to switch its focus to streaming. Similarly, Amazon, having made a success of selling books, had to decide whether to start selling products in unrelated categories. Their decisions to provide cloud services to other companies, make TV shows and movies, and even buy their own jets to compete with traditional logistics providers may seem like obvious choices in retrospect, but at the time they all flew in the face of conventional wisdom. They were tough decisions made by humans in the face of great uncertainty.

Once a year, Jeff Bezos writes a fascinating letter to his shareholders that provides a small window into his thinking. His letter in 2015 was particularly interesting, as it focused on decision making at Amazon.

For Bezos, there are two categories of decisions. Type 1 decisions are the mission-critical, high-impact choices that influence higher-level strategy and can determine your future; Type 2 decisions are the lower-stakes choices that can be reversed if need be. You are better off acting on or even automating Type 2 decisions as quickly as possible. By making a quick decision you can gather the data you need in order to work out if you were correct or not. Amazon's senior leaders typically leave all Type 2 decisions to the teams and individuals below them so they themselves can focus on Type 1 decisions.

Once you know which decisions you should be spending your time on, the next step is to commit to a specific time frame.

In a conversation with Reid Hoffman for his podcast, *Masters of Scale*, former Google CEO Eric Schmidt explained that one of the most effective strategies in speeding up decision making is formalizing meeting agendas. When he and Google's founders, Larry Page and Sergey Brin, formalized their agendas, every employee knew they would get a weekly chance to present a plan to Google's leadership team. As Schmidt put it, "Most large corporations have too many lawyers, too many decision makers, unclear owners, and things congeal, they occur very slowly." This meant that when Google chose to acquire YouTube in a $1.6 billion deal in 2006, the decision process took only ten days.

Some decisions, however, even if you know they are important and they have the full attention of the leadership team, are just intrinsically difficult to make. They are what is known as "wicked problems," and they don't have simple solutions. All you can do is take actions that make a situation better, or worse.

Wicked problems resist conventional analysis, by machines or humans. Sometimes the best way to fully understand their implications is to debate them. The idea of taking opposing positions to get to the core of a difficult issue is a strategy that leaders are sometimes frightened to adopt, especially if they work in an organization where open disagreement or intellectual conflict is discouraged. Contrast this with Netflix, for example, which not only encourages debate but has even gone so far as to have executives debate in front of an audience on big decisions.

A debate is a powerful signal to the rest of the organization that opinions backed by facts are valuable, regardless of where they come from in the organization.

Build an algorithmic brain trust

If the best way to make decisions in ambiguous conditions is to continuously update your knowledge with new data, then how you handle and share data also becomes vital.

There is a collective dimension to knowing how to best leverage algorithms and data in your business, especially if you don't personally have all the requisite expertise or specific domain knowledge to solve a problem. As we saw in the stories of Vanderburg and Shallue, sometimes the most effective way of solving a computational problem is having the right kind of team working on it.

That's where building an algorithmic brain trust at your organization can be a good approach.

The term "brain trust" was popularized by James Kieran, a *New York Times* reporter, to refer to the diverse group of academic advisers that Franklin Roosevelt gathered to assist him during the 1932 presidential campaign. That group helped him develop an economic plan whose programs became the backbone of the New Deal: financial regulation, large-scale relief, and public works programs.

Creating an algorithmic brain trust can be as simple as scheduling a regular meeting of the right people. Ideally, in large organizations this might be a combination of business unit leaders, the data science team, and those responsible for AI and machine learning. If you work in a smaller company or are a freelancer, you can assemble your own mastermind group of outside experts and people with similar challenges who can guide you on your journey.

Tokyo in spring is one of the most beautiful places on the planet. Cherry blossoms called *sakura* transform the streets with pink clouds of flowers, all the more beautiful for their transience; the blooms often last for merely a week before they fall like pastel snow. During one sakura season I visited Japan's leading e-commerce company, Rakuten, and met with Takuya Kitagawa, its chief digital officer.

Kitagawa was in charge of a new centralized data division at the business called the Global Data Supervisory Department, whose role was to bring together the analytics and data platform teams. Rakuten has 30 million customers and is also the country's number one credit card company, with 12 million users. The Rakuten rewards program has allowed the company to effectively drive promotions and customer behaviors within its various business units and brands. It should come as no surprise, then, that data is considered the lifeblood of the business.

Despite its digital DNA, Rakuten used to be a very sales-driven organization. In its early days, new employees were expected to serve their time in the call center and prove that they could close deals. There was a rumor that phones were tied onto people's hands until they had made their first sale. Over the last few years, Rakuten has transformed itself from a sales-obsessed company to a data-focused one.

The company's vision, Kitagawa explained, was to become a membership company to compete with Amazon and Facebook. Rather than having its brands trying to market to each consumer individually for different products, the new strategy was to create a universe of brand offers, which could then be selectively marketed to members. In Kitagawa's view, the key to getting that right would be algorithms and machine learning.

Rakuten therefore created its own algorithmic brain trust. Every quarter, all the senior leaders gather to discuss data. Each division has its own chief data officer who shares at these meetings how they will use data more effectively and what new data initiatives have been successful. Data experts from the platform then also present their findings and new approaches. The idea is to create an environment that allows both business and technology leaders to see new patterns and to potentially apply learnings from one division to another.

As I left our meeting, I noticed a sign listing the company's five core values. Value #3 contained three English words and one Japanese word. It read: "hypothesize—practice—validate—*shikumika!*"

"What does *shikumika* mean?" I asked Kitagawa, as he walked me past a dense cluster of meeting rooms, each furnished with items made by local artisans and available for purchase on the Rakuten platform.

"*Shikumika* is to systemize," explained Kitagawa. "In practice, that means to learn ideas from one part of the business, turn them into a system, and apply them elsewhere."

An effective algorithmic brain trust is the perfect example of twenty-first century *shikumika*: take ideas and learnings about the effective use of data from one part of the business, transform them into an algorithmic system, and apply that system elsewhere.

Experiment to find questions, not answers

Central to our discussion of embracing uncertainty so far has been the value of an empirical process approach. In the scientific community, the word "empirical" means based on experiment or observation. Experiments are a valuable way to gather data, but they play an even more important role for smart leaders: they make it possible to frame better questions.

Running experiments has become a cliché of modern-day management. Facebook CEO Mark Zuckerberg says the company conducts tens of thousands of experiments at any given time. The growth team at Airbnb claims to run over 700 experiments a week, and if you count randomized A/B testing, then pretty much every digital company from Netflix to Google is running millions and millions of experiments concurrently.

In an algorithmic organization, experiments don't provide answers; their intent is not just to prove whether bold or italic on a landing page will sell more product. They validate questions; they are used to demonstrate that typographic choices are a key variable in sales growth.

Finding unexpected correlations between variables is one of the reasons that unsupervised machine learning holds a lot of promise for the future of smart strategy. With AI, these experiments can now happen on a scale that was previously impossible.

The most valuable aspect of decision making for algorithmic leaders is seeking out non-obvious decisions to make or bold questions to ask that have not occurred to anyone else. Rather than replacing decision makers, algorithms in this context actually help leaders focus on the issues worth further exploration.

Good decisions should be difficult. Their difficulty reflects the challenging nature of the topics and issues they relate to; they require strong cognitive skills if you are to arrive at a good solution. If your decision doesn't seem difficult to make, you are probably not asking the right questions.

You can train an algorithm to spot financial fraud, but it won't tell you whether or not you should even be in the payments business. You can run randomized tests to see which of your email campaigns work best, but that data won't tell you the value of having a human personally calling a high-value client. You can decide to just make a single pilot episode of a TV show as an experiment to see if people like it, but you will never know what might have happened if you had just commissioned the entire season up front and given it time to find an audience.

Decision making in the algorithmic age is a moving target. The boundaries of what can and should be automated will shift constantly as AI improves and more data becomes available. Digital platforms will offer you endless opportunities to run experiments on your users. Some of these will be acceptable and even welcome, especially when they lead to better experiences. Others, where consent is ambiguous or third parties are involved, may be problematic— or even illegal.

Navigating the new world of algorithmic decision making will not be easy. Not only is it challenging to identify and focus on the right decisions to make, but also, you have to create the right context and systems to do so.

In the end, being an effective algorithmic leader means finding mechanisms and mindsets to cope with uncertainty, both by yourself and with your teams. So, isolate the factors that really matter, have a sense of the odds, check your assumptions, make a decision, and then reevaluate when new information comes to light. And, most importantly, learn to love uncertainty.

SUMMARY

1 Adopting a probabilistic mindset allows you to be better pre-pared for the uncertainties and complexities of the algorithmic age. Rather than trying to be always right, probabilistic thinkers instead try to be less wrong with time.

2 Your organization's ability to rapidly assimilate new data and insights will determine how well it manages uncertainty. Without a smarter way of running meetings, you will compromise your abil-ity to effectively share information, manage projects, and make decisions.

3 Conducting a decision audit will allow you to distinguish the deci-sions that really matter from the ones that can be automated or delegated. The fewer unimportant decisions that humans need to make, the more we can fully engage with the important ones.

4 Assembling an algorithmic brain trust or your own mastermind group is a good way to share and systemize the use of data and AI in your organization.

5 The real value of running experiments is not to find solutions but to uncover better questions. AI will not automate innovation; it will help leaders focus on the issues and ideas worthy of further exploration.

QUESTION

How do you reconcile a culture of experimentation with the need for developing a long-term vision for the future?

PART II

CHANGE

YOUR

WORK

MAKE CULTURE YOUR OPERATING SYSTEM

"The technology is the easy part. The hard part is figuring out the social and institutional structures around the technology."

JOHN SEELY BROWN

Put principles before processes

Work is changing. Not just because we have new technology to drive efficiency and automation, but also because the nature of business itself is becoming more complex, unpredictable, and dynamic.

Strangely enough, the more we automate work and decision making, the more important it becomes to thoughtfully manage and support the remaining human-based activities. Underestimate the creativity and agility of the human mind at your own risk! Even as AI improves, there will always be tasks, decisions, and activities that machines cannot accomplish and that humans must take on. And in fact, as everything else becomes automated, the human-reliant tasks actually increase in importance.

So how should algorithmic leaders manage their teams in this new environment? Do we need highly structured workflows, performance indicators, and processes? Or simply some fluid principles to guide behavior?

These are important questions to consider, because they go to the heart of what separates twenty-first-century companies from twentieth-century ones. You might think the difference is nothing more than technology. Software vendors will promise you greater productivity, collaboration, and employee engagement if you upgrade your systems. If only it were that simple!

You can't buy your way into the twenty-first century. Sure, you can spend millions on upgrading your systems, but nothing will change if you don't put in the hard work of thinking about how your people should interact with each other, solve problems, and generate ideas. Technology may have changed the hardware of your business, but culture is your true operating system.

Great corporate culture isn't easy to create. And I'm not going to tell you how to do it. It is something you and your team need to figure out on your own. Literally thousands of books have been written on the subject. You could read all of them and still not know what to do. The reason for that is simple: company culture is like the culture of a country. Paris, Texas, will never be Paris, France.

The true secret of successful cultural change is finding and augmenting the behaviors, patterns, and mindsets that are already working for you, rather than trying to superimpose the values of another company onto your own. That said, while you ought to avoid blindly adopting another company's approach, you can learn something from the experiences and struggles of other algorithmic leaders. While some factors that affect workplace culture will be familiar to you, they need to be reconsidered in the context of data and AI.

A good starting point is the question of control. Do you design a perfect model of what high performance looks like and get your teams to conform to that? Or do you give people the freedom to do what they think is best?

One of the most influential documents on how to manage people in an algorithmic era came from Netflix. Shared millions of times on SlideShare, the 124-page document called *Netflix Culture: Freedom & Responsibility* was written by Patty McCord, the former head of talent at the company, who spent fourteen years in the job. The Netflix Culture Deck, as it became known, was called "the most important document ever to come out of the Valley" by Facebook COO Sheryl Sandberg.

The deck is worth a read. Some of its ideas were developed further by McCord in *Powerful*, where she explains that the fundamental lesson they learned at Netflix is that the elaborate, cumbersome system for managing people developed in the twentieth century is no longer appropriate for survival in the twenty-first. However, rather than creating a complex new model for managing people (like Holacracy), they did the opposite. They kept removing policies, processes, and procedures so that people could get stuff done, guided by their own judgment.

In McCord's view, too many companies try to patch their command-and-control system of decision making with talk of "employee engagement" and "empowering people," offering bonuses and pay tied to annual performance reviews, or "fun" workplace activities. The false assumption here is that people must be incentivized in order to commit themselves fully to their work and that they need to be told what to do. Netflix discovered that by embedding a core set of behaviors in its people, and then giving them the freedom to practice them, its teams would be naturally motivated, proactive, and ultimately successful.

Principles rather than *processes* are what matter.

Principles can't be vague mission statements. They have to be concrete enough to be useful, but fluid enough to adapt to a wide variety of circumstances. Just coming up with a list of motherhood statements will not lead to culture change. Even Enron and Bear Stearns had their own set of values, for all the good it did them in the end. Amazon's 14 Leadership Principles work because they are a codification of useful behaviors that are already practiced daily at the company. Take a moment to look them up. They make for interesting reading and discussion with your colleagues.

While the story about Jeff Bezos writing down his founding fourteen principles on a napkin when he started Amazon is probably apocryphal, there is no doubt that the principles have been adopted enthusiastically by his leaders and teams.

For example, take Principle #1: Customer Obsession. The exact wording is this: "Leaders start with the customer and work backward. They work vigorously to earn and keep customer trust. Although leaders pay attention to competitors, they obsess over customers."

Many companies express similar views about customers, but without going to the lengths that Amazon does in bringing its values to life. For example, whenever Amazon is planning a new product, the team involved has to come up with a PR-FAQ, an imaginary pseudo press release describing the new product and a list of the kinds of questions that customers might have about it.

Other values, like Principle #13: Have Backbone; Disagree and Commit, might be less obvious, but they are similarly tied to the decision-making culture at Amazon. In a letter to shareholders on the topic of Principle #13, Bezos explained that rather than having his team waste time trying to convince him to make a decision that he disagrees with, he backs them and gives them the chance to prove him wrong. As an example, he describes a decision to approve a particular Amazon Studios original program.

"I told the team my view: debatable whether it would be interesting enough, complicated to produce, the business terms aren't that good, and we have lots of other opportunities. They had a completely different opinion and wanted to go ahead. I wrote back right away with 'I disagree and commit and hope it becomes the most watched thing we've ever made.' Consider how much slower this decision cycle would have been if the team had actually had to convince me rather than simply get my commitment."

The most important part of governing by principles rather than processes is doing just that: you have to stand behind them. Too many traditional leaders claim to serve the customer, or claim that they encourage innovative thinking, but when the opportunity comes to back their teams and trust their judgment, they indirectly sabotage their ideas by not providing the right resources, support, or affirmation.

Be a gardener, not a prison guard

Daniel Hulme started his company with a depressing thought: he calculated that he had only 700 months to live.

At the time, Hulme was in his early twenties and finishing his doctorate in optimization at University College London. From a young age, Hulme had been curious about how the universe worked and what it meant to be human, which had led him to research complexity theory and artificial intelligence. But it was his morbid thinking on the fleeting nature of time that led him to look past programming to the great philosophers—the Greeks, the Stoics, the existentialists—for some compelling answers. He discovered in those ancient writings a universal principle that still holds true: the ultimate meaning of life is to maximize happiness and minimize its suffering. In short, the meaning of life is to *maximize good.*

Thinking about that equation led Hulme to realize that academic life was not going to be a satisfying way to solve real-world problems and reduce suffering in the world. So he created Satalia, a company that started out as a conduit for academic algorithms to be applied more broadly in the world. But secretly, Satalia was also a vehicle for Hulme to understand what motivated people and made them happy, to learn the dynamics of science, commerce, society, and economics. Through data and code, he hoped to gain a glimpse into how the universe worked.

When Hulme came to visit me at my place in London, I asked him about the values he had embedded in the culture of his company. About eighty people worked at Satalia without managers, hierarchies, or key performance indicators. Hulme described it as everyone being completely free to do whatever they wanted. Even if you are an intern at Satalia, you can expense anything you want. That's not to say that it is an anarchical commune full of kombucha-drinking hipsters chilling out at the company's expense. Behind that layer of trust is a sophisticated algorithmic infrastructure. The company uses machine learning to understand how people are connected across the organization and pinpoint who has the right expertise to be making certain decisions.

To illustrate his model in action, Hulme explained that his company recently went through an exercise where everybody in the company made public recommendations for their own salary. Everybody then voted on whether those salaries should be reduced, increased, or kept the same. If you were voting on someone else's salary, the weight of your vote was a function of how closely you had worked with that person over the past year and how highly regarded you were as a strategic decision maker.

For Hulme, the organizational design of Satalia is an attempt to figure out how you might decentralize and redistribute decision making across an organization, while also making those decisions visible. As an example, one of the insights from the pay review experiment was that women at the company were undervaluing themselves. When presented with this information, the rest of the organization voted to increase the women's salaries. That kind of decision would have been hidden in a traditional organization, where it is likely that salaries are not transparent and a manager is making salary-related decisions.

Hulme believes that the key to success in a decentralized organization is for leaders to act as humble gardeners rather than prison guards. The job of a leader is not to enforce their views and ensure compliance, but rather to provide nutrients and the space to allow things to grow. In an organizational context, that means giving people information and resources, and allowing them to figure out how to allocate their time and attention in a way that benefits both them and the company.

Ali Parsa, the founder of Babylon Health, is an algorithmic leader we will meet later in this book. When I interviewed him, he expressed a similar view. For Parsa, acting like a gardener was not so much an expression of humility but rather an act of sheer practicality when faced with exponential rates of growth.

"Most corporations are managed by a small number of people at the top," Parsa explained. "That works if you're going to improve by 10 per cent or 15 per cent. But if you're growing at 100 per cent, 200 per cent, or 300 per cent a year, it is impossible for any human being to keep all of this in their head. So then the job is not being the puppet master but a gardener. You need to create an environment in which every plant can grow on its own."

Curiously enough, Parsa's favorite example of the power of decentralized control was not from current times. He was fascinated by the growth of the British Empire, which expanded globally over a hundred-year period until it managed over 20 per cent of the land on the planet without any direct control from the center. Buccaneers, tradesmen, and merchant seamen were given lots of delegated decision making in a highly self-organized fashion.

That is, until they changed their management model. One of the principal causes of the collapse of the British Empire was, in Parsa's opinion, the invention of the telegram. When messages went from being transported by ships, with a send and receive time of six months, to a mere six minutes, everything fell apart. Because, as Parsa explained with a wry grin, the center suddenly started to micromanage.

Design teams to succeed

Leaders have long enjoyed tinkering with team design. Steve Jobs was notorious for insisting that meetings should be small groups of smart people. He had no compunction about letting someone know if they weren't needed. Jeff Bezos's two-pizza team rule was his attempt to stop people wasting time on pursuing consensus. Even while granting teams the freedom to manage themselves, algorithmic leaders will often experiment with the design and structure of how people work.

An interesting example of team design in action is Johnson & Johnson Vision, the world's leading manufacturer of contact lenses. A few years back, J&J Vision announced its intention to expand beyond contact lenses and become a global leader in eye health by 2030, which would require an increase of $4 billion a year in its current turnover, significantly higher than the category growth rate of 5 per cent. While part of this growth target would come from selling more of their traditional eye products, even more would need to come from acquisitions and innovations in the area of eye health, such as cataracts and glaucoma treatment.

Having been invited to speak on the future of algorithmic leadership a few times at J&J, I got to know one of their senior leaders, Aldo Denti, who was VP of Global Franchise Development. Denti grew up in Canada. His father was a doctor, and his mother a nurse. When Denti was just sixteen, his brother passed away from leukemia, a devastating event for his family that would end up directing him into pursuing a career in healthcare and eventually joining J&J.

With such an audacious goal to reach by 2030, Denti realized that dramatic changes were required. J&J needed a new way to work. Amazon and Walmart were both already making early moves into the healthcare space. Nike had acquired Zodiac, a leading consumer data analytics firm. Domino's had become a technology company by focusing on technology-enabled customer experiences. Even Pepsi had built a 200-person e-commerce team to compete with Amazon. From Denti's viewpoint, all of those companies and their teams, as well as their traditional competitors, had become more agile, adaptive, and data-driven than his own teams at J&J.

In 2014, when Denti first started thinking about the problem of team design, the business was challenged by a hierarchical mindset and a heavily siloed operating model. Even though there was pressure for brands to be more consumer-centric and to orchestrate their communications across digital platforms, J&J was just not organized in a way that allowed the different functions to speak to each other.

Denti first tried to reboot innovation by trialing a program called the three-legged stool model, which brought R&D, marketing, and the supply chain team together to accelerate the innovation cycle and deliver a brand new daily disposable contact lens in eighteen months. Without needing to wait for consensus from across the company, this small, dynamic team achieved its goal, saving time on a project that had been initially estimated as requiring an additional two years to complete.

With that success under its belt, J&J launched a new project. This time it created a small, cross-functional team to explore emerging technologies, like photochromic contact lenses. The initiative didn't work. The team was neither fully resourced nor fully empowered. There wasn't executive alignment on what the team had to deliver, and the team didn't have the right cross-functional members. There were also some gaps in leadership. As a result, little was achieved. For Denti, the key learning from the experience was that without the right resourcing and alignment of team members and executive sponsors, there is no chance of success.

Reconciling what they had learned from their two experiments, Denti and his team put together what they called the "pod" team concept, with a focus on beauty consumers in Asia. J&J knew that in Asia, millennial beauty seekers had a different outlook than they did in the West. In the East, the focus is on personal expression and beauty amplification, rather than freedom through wearing prescription lenses. J&J had never really been able to capture those particular consumers, so it wanted to accelerate that aspect of their business, not just through innovation but also by changing the engagement model to be more digital, using influencers and social platforms.

The beauty pod that Denti formed was a success. With a core team of twelve members, the pod had executive alignment around a clear target: develop new contact lenses through the beauty channel that would also benefit the Acuvue brand. This time, Denti assembled the right group of people, including someone from R&D, local marketers, and a supply chain expert all reporting to a single person (an experienced marketer from Japan). They gave this pod leader finance and communications support. The beauty pod was almost like a pop-up business unit designed to reach an aspirational goal, with a fixed time limit.

"What you also need to understand," explained Denti as he finished sharing his story with me, "is that the primary impetus for the pod structure was our realization that algorithms, AI, and machine learning would be at the center of our new way of working. And so as a result of that, we said if we want data to really live, then we would have to surround the data with people that can not only extract it but also do something interesting with it.

"In the old world, data would sit in analytics or insights. You would go to your data department and try to extract what you needed, and then go back to your functional day job, such as marketing, and try to do something with it. But that's not the way the new world works.

"The new way demands that you put the data scientist, the algorithm, and the machine at the center of what you're doing. Set the proposition that you're trying to solve as the aspiration. Then resource that aspiration with the people that can extract the data and action it. Our pod system is built around data science and machine learning. Every single pod must have its tie-in to data and data science as a principle of the pod design."

Set the stage for smart ideas

In mid-2016, IBM started calling people back to the office.

Jeff Smith, IBM's CIO, was determined to make his company more agile, which to his mind meant that more work had to be done by small teams constantly collaborating on projects and using data to make decisions. That meant that people would need to spend more time in the office.

Many IBM employees had worked from home successfully for years, but when the company researched the most disruptive, original, and successful teams, they discovered they were generally those that were based in a single location. In Smith's words,

"Leaders have to be with the squads and the squads have to be in a location."

Remote work had been a feature of life at IBM for a long time. Remote terminals had been installed in some employees' homes as far back as the 1980s; in 2009, when many companies were still insisting their staff turn up to a campus or office for work, 40 per cent of IBM's 386,000 global employees worked from home. But at a time when the company required fresh ideas and more disruptive innovation, its leaders were hoping that bringing people back together might deliver the productivity gains it needed.

IBM was not alone in its attempts to reboot the workplace. Packing smart people into one place as a catalyst for creativity is not a new idea. Even at the scale of cities, there is evidence that concentration leads to more fruitful connections. Influential twentieth-century urban theorists like Jane Jacobs and economists like Robert Lucas Jr. argued, for example, that dense packs of talented workers boost local economies and innovative thinking. Could algorithms and data also assist leaders in optimizing for these types of outcomes?

On a visit to Seattle, I spent some time with Dan Anthony and Sean McKeever, two architects and leaders of NBBJ's design computation team. NBBJ is one of the world's leading design firms, used by technology companies like Google and Amazon in the US, and Alipay and Tencent in China.

NBBJ is increasingly using algorithmic, computational design frameworks to help its clients reinvent their workspaces. This approach, known as parametric design, uses algorithms and computer models to simulate how a building's occupants will use a space. Typically, you might use a parametric model to link geometry with data to address specific requirements such as the kinds of views available from different offices. NBBJ has taken the idea a few steps further with its Human Experience Toolkit.

Working with neuroscientists and psychologists, NBBJ is embedding behavioral insights as variables in workplace models. A floorplan, for example, can now be algorithmically optimized for its collaborative potential, based on how easy it is for team members to see each other.

Alternatively, you might optimize for prospect and refuge, a human behavior theory in anthropology and neuroscience that posits that the part of our brain that evolved from our days living on the savannah still influences our response to the workplace. Humans feel safer and more comfortable when we can survey the area around us (prospect) and find a good cave to hide in (refuge). Using algorithmic design, these insights into human performance can be embedded and brought to life in our physical work environments.

Design is relevant not just to the way that you put teams together, but also to the environments in which you house those teams. You have to literally set the stage for success and smart thinking. But sometimes, to really transform a company, you have to go further than a simple office redesign. You have to find a way to hack your culture.

Use data to hack your culture

As a leader, Jim Barksdale is a contradictory mix of Southern charm and ruthless business acumen. He served as COO at FedEx and CEO at AT&T Wireless, and probably most famously, he nurtured Netscape from its beginnings as the first dotcom startup to its spectacular sale to AOL. One of my favorite quotes is attributed to him: "If we have the data, let's look at the data. If all we have are opinions, let's just go with mine."

Changing behavior in an organization is not easy unless you can have a fact-based conversation about it. If you try to transform your culture with only anecdotes, tribal knowledge, and opinions to back you up, the chances are it won't go so well.

That's why algorithmic organizations are starting to use data to understand what makes their teams and people successful. Google, in particular, has started conducting long-range studies on performance (see the discussion of Project Aristotle in chapter 4), but it is far from unique.

When Ben Waber first started his PhD research at the MIT Media Lab, he came across some extant research that showed that based on changes in the way people speak, you could predict who was going to win a salary negotiation, how a venture capitalist might rate a business plan pitch, or how successful a romantic date might be. This research was not looking at the words themselves, but rather at things like changes in tone of voice, and how quickly or how loudly people speak.

The research fascinated Waber and his colleagues. He started to wonder what might happen if you tried to modify those signals, so he created a program where you could feed in speech, and the software would ramp up or tone down attributes like persuasion levels or attraction levels. To run this experiment in the lab, Waber and his colleagues created wearable sensors that resembled a kind of oversized employee ID badge.

One day, a professor from the MIT Sloan School of Management came by the lab and was intrigued by the team's ID sensors. He told them that he had been studying a large bank in Germany, collecting all their email data and giving people surveys every day about what they were doing. On seeing the ID badges, he wondered whether he could start collecting data about the way that employees interacted face to face in the workplace and use that to predict performance, job satisfaction, and other operating measures. The professor asked Waber whether he might like to help him with his project in Germany.

Waber was interested in the offer, but also nervous. In the laboratory, they had only managed to get their sensors to work continuously for a total of two hours at a time. How well would they fare in an actual workplace, where the badges would need to be worn all the time?

Nevertheless, Waber and his colleagues accepted the challenge and went to Germany. They had to work right up to the last minute—in their hotel room, not a lab—to finish the operating system of the badges on time. As the data started coming in, almost four gigabytes per person per day, they decided to pick something simple to analyze.

Waber and his team started to track who was talking to whom in the company, and what the bank's social network looked like. And then, using just those metrics, they tried to predict subjective and quantitative ratings of performance for different employees as well as self-reported job satisfaction levels. A classic example of probabilistic problem solving in action!

To everyone's surprise, the data from even these simple employee interactions proved to be an incredibly accurate predictor of performance. In particular, the cohesiveness of a group, or how much people talked to each other, was by far the strongest predictor of performance across almost every attribute being measured. When the leaders of this multibillion-euro bank read the research report, they instantly kicked off an entire reorganization of the business, based on the analysis, as Waber puts it, of "a bunch of grad students who had just written up an academic paper."

Waber subsequently co-founded, with Daniel Olguin, Taemie Kim, Tuomas Jaanu, and MIT Professor Alex Pentland, Humanyze, a behavioral analytics company that uses wearable sensors to transform company culture and operating models. When I asked him about how that European bank had implemented the data from his team's findings into its organizational structure, he explained that many traditional companies rely on an org chart that provides incomplete information.

"An org chart might tell you who does what," said Waber, "but of course, there's another side of it, which is, who needs to be working with whom? They're related, but they're different. And so what that bank did was to look at which people needed to strategically work together. Once they knew that, they could put them on the same team or in the same part of the organization."

Companies collect a lot of data, both deliberately and unintentionally, about how their employees work, interact with colleagues, and relate to customers. And yet, despite all this data, in Waber's view, there are basic questions that almost no companies today can answer. For example, how much do sales teams talk to engineering teams? How much should a store assistant talk to a customer? Although these are core issues, most leaders can generally only guess about what actually happens, or what the right approach should be.

For Waber, the key to cultural transformation and smarter operational decisions is to gather and analyze the granular data about how people work. Even a decision like setting up a new office can be better understood by looking at employee networks. Typically, those kinds of decisions are based on costs; however, if you can actually measure which people need to work together and how they communicate, you can make your operational decisions about co-location much more accurately and effectively.

As an example, Waber told me a story about one of his clients, the Boston Consulting Group (BCG), which was planning to move 1,000 people in the New York area to a new office. The company had certain behavioral objectives that it wanted to achieve with this new workspace, including ensuring that its software developers, who built custom analytics and programs for its clients, could spend at least 40 per cent of their time doing focused work without interruptions.

Unfortunately, as soon as the teams moved into their new office, the amount of focused work time actually dropped to 20 per cent. After reviewing the data from Waber's smart lanyards, the company realized that it was related to the design of the office. The programmers were sitting right next to the staff canteen. Every time someone went for a coffee, they stopped for a chat. After BCG's leaders saw the data, they put up fabric walls. By the following week, the focused work time had almost doubled.

Creating a cultural operating system that allows your best people to thrive is not for the faint-hearted. It is not something that can be achieved by upgrading your technology or blindly copying the approach of another company. What works for you and your team will be unique to you and your situation.

The good news is that the basis for your future success is already with you, hidden among the interactions and behaviors of your best, most innovative co-workers. With the right values, team design, mentoring, work environment, algorithmic analysis, and data, you may even be able to scale that up to include everyone else.

SUMMARY

1 Technology may have changed the hardware of your business, but culture is your true operating system. Creating an effective culture requires identifying and nurturing the right set of principles, rather than controlling people through processes.

2 Algorithmic leaders can leverage data and machine learning to create a more autonomous and decentralized environment for their teams to work in. It is better to be a gardener who provides a fertile environment for growth than a prison guard whose job is to ensure compliance.

3 Clever team design is good way to accelerate cultural change. Aldo Denti's pod teams at Johnson & Johnson are an example of how team structures can support innovation, agile management, and rapid development when breakthrough growth is required.

4 Where people work is as important as how they work. In the future we will combine data science and computational design with behavioral science and anthropology in order to algorithmically reinvent our workspaces.

5 It is difficult to embark on a journey of cultural transformation if you can't have a fact-based conversation about what needs to change. Look for ways to collect data on how you work, and use this as a basis for hacking your culture.

QUESTION

Which aspects of your culture are the most supportive of your transformation and which ones are likely to hold you back?

DON'T WORK, DESIGN WORK

"Digital recognizes no digital business unit."
SATYA NADELLA, CEO OF MICROSOFT

Challenge your raison d'être

The job of an algorithmic leader is not to work. Their real job is to design work.

Rather than worrying about how well they are performing as measured by standard business metrics, algorithmic leaders should take a step back and consider the nature of the work itself.

When traditional leaders measure themselves and others, they inadvertently use metrics that preserve, rather than challenge, the raison d'être of the status quo: *Are we meeting our targets? How are we tracking against our key performance indicators? Is the team exceeding expectations? Is the employee engagement survey up or down this month? How about our Net Promoter Score?*

Unfortunately, a big part of "getting work done" for the last fifty years has translated as standardizing activities and outcomes to establish benchmarks against which to measure people. Perhaps the most controversial of these was the Vitality Curve, pioneered by Jack Welch at General Electric in the 1980s.

Welch's Vitality Curve, also known as a stack or forced ranking (or more colloquially, the rank and yank method), is a management practice that requires an entire company to be sorted into three groups. Welch would ask his leaders to periodically rank their teams into "A," "B," and "C" players. The "A" group, comprising the top 20 per cent, was considered the best, and its members were promoted and given higher compensation. The next 70 per cent, the "B" players, were considered as working adequately, and presumably were allowed to keep their jobs. As for the "C" players, or the bottom 10 per cent, Welch demanded that these be immediately fired.

Leaving aside the negative impacts on employee culture and the potential for discrimination and political vendettas, the biggest problem with the Vitality Curve, and why it was discontinued even at GE, was that it was ultimately pseudoscientific. Rather than identify top talent, the Vitality Curve simply confused the issue of what good work should be in the first place.

Welch's guidelines for what made for an "A" player were notoriously vague. "A" players were, in his opinion, "filled with passion," committed to "making things happen," and blessed with "lots of runway ahead of them"; they had "very high energy levels" and lots of charisma; and they could "energize others around common goals." They sound more like a psychological test for uncovering workplace sociopaths than indicators of high performance.

Unfortunately, it doesn't really matter whether you use an abstract concept like "A" players or a metric like employee engagement; you will face the same problem. Your metrics are a snapshot of your organization's priorities at a specific point in time. But what happens when things change?

Part of being an algorithmic leader means being able to constantly step back from the task, activity, or mission at hand and ask yourself: *Is this the smartest way of doing this?* Rather than just trying to improve a score, time, or some other indicator, an algorithmic leader takes a meta-perspective and questions the ultimate premise of the job itself.

The question you should be asking is not *Are we getting results?* but *Do we have the right approach?*

When Joshua Browder started to drive in his late teens, he suddenly found himself with lots of parking fines. In his view, many of those fines were entirely unfair. Some of the parking signs were confusing, and others were not even visible. Browder decided to challenge some of the fines, and was subsequently surprised at the lack of free resources to help him do so. Sure, there were some dubious lawyers available who could appeal the fines for you, but they wanted half the cost of the ticket as compensation.

Browder was well equipped to handle a challenge like this. He had taught himself to code at age twelve and knew how to look at problems in a structured way. (He was, you might say, a natural computational thinker.) As he started to appeal the tickets, he noticed the highly formulaic nature of the process. There were set questions and responses that led to more questions. In other words, a process that lent itself to automation.

By now he was a student at Stanford University, and one night he found some time between midnight and 3:00 a.m. to create a website that he called DoNotPay. His application was a simple robot lawyer designed to help people challenge the very kinds of fines he had incurred himself. The website went viral, and since its launch in 2015, it has not only saved drivers millions of dollars in fines but also expanded to offering other consumer-help services, from helping people impacted by the Equifax breach launch automated lawsuits, to getting refunds on flight tickets when prices drop.

Browder is one of those rare people whose Wikipedia page has links to equally famous members of his immediate family, all of whom had been influential figures in mathematics, politics, and even espionage.

His father, Bill Browder, was the co-founder of Hermitage Capital Management, an investment fund that was once the largest foreign investor in Russia during that country's first wave of privatization. He was eventually kicked out of Russia for being a threat to national security (allegedly as a result of his exposing corruption). Felix Browder, Josh's grandfather, won the National Medal of Science in 1999. Felix was a child prodigy in mathematics who entered MIT at age seventeen, pioneered work in nonlinear functional analysis, and famously had a library of 35,000 books. Felix's father, Joshua's great-grandfather, was just as influential. Earl Russell Browder was the leader of the Communist Party in the United States and a vocal activist for workers' rights through the Great Depression. He even ran for president of the United States twice, and, it would later emerge, served as a recruiter of KGB intelligence operatives in the 1940s.

What makes Josh Browder's story an interesting one is that his mindset and approach represent precisely the kind of strategy that an algorithmic leader should adopt when identifying and attacking the formulaic workflows inside organizations. Looking for a smarter way to do things is only the first step on your journey of transformation.

Digital transformation requires you to not only automate your processes but also reimagine what you do. In some ways, this is an extension of the logic in Michael Hammer and James Champy's 1993 book *Reengineering the Corporation*. In that groundbreaking book, the authors argued that companies need to step back from their processes and focus on the actual objectives that they want to achieve. Leaders could then study the workflows and figure out the tasks that are required to achieve those objectives. The question of whether computers should be involved should only come in after that analysis had been completed. In fact, in 1990, Hammer had written an article with the subtitle "Don't automate, obliterate."

Digital transformation is a more sophisticated and intricate process of change and demands more from leaders than business process management (BPM) ever did. Ultimately, BPM was about streamlining and automating rules-based work. Digital transformation begins with the customer and asks leaders to consider, given the data, algorithms, and digital platforms at their disposal, how they might fundamentally reimagine the entire customer experience.

Hammer and Champy argue that we should simply eliminate processes that don't add value. My view is that algorithmic leaders need to go beyond this step and fundamentally reimagine their objectives and processes from a customer perspective.

People shouldn't need to understand an organization's underlying structure to get things done. Whether you are signing up for a car loan or insurance policy, or even paying a utility bill, the process should be seamless and intuitive. The same applies to employees. Everything from ordering a new computer to onboarding a customer to promoting an employee can be transformed with predictive analytics so that decisions can find the people who need to make them, rather than workers having to find work to do.

The good news is that it is getting easier for leaders, even without technical expertise, to redesign what they do. Work is moving from a very unstructured activity in which email and spreadsheets were used to communicate and solve problems to something more structured, a system in which leaders can design and combine modules of automated interactions.

The "work design" approach was pioneered in IT, where the sheer volume of help requests led IT professionals to create structured ways for users to request tickets and to have an automated way of handling those requests. Elsewhere in business—for example, marketing, finance, or HR—there are still many unstructured ways of working, whether it be calling, leaving notes, or having meetings or informally collaborating. In an algorithmic organization, the more activity that can be captured by the system, the smarter your algorithms can become, and the easier it is for smart leaders to design better ways of working.

Find the scaled-up solution

Taking time to think about the smarter, algorithmic way of doing things will also help you uncover potential ways of delivering a scaled-up solution.

Analogue leaders look for a profitable way to run their business, to make a reasonable return on people and assets. Algorithmic leaders try to design a model that allows them to deliver their service on a truly global scale.

The story of Babylon Health, one of the world's leading AI healthcare providers, is a powerful illustration of the benefits of using algorithms to achieve a scaled-up solution. At a time when many healthcare providers are struggling to care for the residents of their home countries, online-based Babylon has started providing AI-based health services in every corner of the world, from Rwanda to Saudi Arabia, China to the UK. How did it establish this reach? The best way to understand Babylon's journey toward global scale is to start with the story of its founder, Ali Parsa.

When I visited Parsa at his London, UK, offices in Chelsea, he explained how his company was a reflection of his life and experiences. Parsa was born in Tehran and, while still a child, moved to a beachside community in the Caspian Sea region with his family. His father was a civil engineer and his mother a government cartographer. While life was relatively calm and peaceful in his local neighborhood in the late seventies, elsewhere in the country change was afoot, and demonstrations and protests against the government were starting to intensify.

By 1979, the Shah, the last Persian monarch, was sent into exile, and the country voted by national referendum to become an Islamic republic with Ayatollah Khomeini as the Supreme Leader. A young teenager at the time, Parsa remembered joining the people on the streets to celebrate, as the excitement of change surged through the country. But as the revolution began to affect daily life, and universities, schools, and other institutions began to shut down, he realized that in order to get an education, he would have to leave. So, by himself, without knowing anyone, and with little money and no English, he emigrated to London. He was just sixteen.

During the revolution, when the schools were closed, Parsa had become used to learning at home. Needing to find a path into the education system in the UK, he did the same. For two years, he studied at home, teaching himself English and preparing for the exams that would admit him into university. At age eighteen, he enrolled at University College London to study civil engineering. He eventually gained a PhD in engineering physics.

Parsa soon discovered that having a PhD and being an academic was prestigious but not financially rewarding. He therefore built a media and events business as a sideline to help cover his living costs; a few years later, he was lucky enough to sell it. During the acquisition process, he was amazed to learn that the banker leading the sale was earning much more in per hour terms than the people who had built the company. So he became a banker. And hated it. In his words, the builder in him was frustrated at the project nature of the work and the all-consuming focus on money. All of his childhood had been about building things. His father designed and built roads and factories; his mother made beautiful, detailed maps.

Around the time that Parsa was looking for an idea to devote himself to, he had to undergo a series of surgeries on his knee. He was shocked at the conditions in even the highest-status private hospitals in London. The average UK hospital at the time was fifty years old if it was private, and about seventy if it was public. So, he started putting together a plan to build a portfolio of hospitals that were modern, equipped with the latest technology, and run based on the newest management techniques. He called this new business Circle and persuaded Lehman Brothers and the Royal Bank of Scotland to give him $500 million. Then the 2008 crash hit, and his financiers backed out.

Suddenly, without the money to build, Parsa and his team had to change direction. They decided to run existing hospitals that were underperforming. At first, the British National Health Service (NHS) gave him only a small day surgical unit to run. When that started to deliver positive results, they gave him the UK's largest day surgical unit. Eventually, Parsa's team became the very first group outside of the NHS to manage an entire hospital.

That hospital, Hinchingbrooke, was one of the worst-performing hospitals in the UK, and in order to turn it around, Parsa realized that he would need to ensure that everyone who worked there owned the problem. So he made all the staff co-owners. He took 50 per cent of his shares in Circle and donated them to the hospital staff. "Now we're partners," he told them. "So, everything we improve, we improve together."

Despite his success at reinventing the operating model of his hospitals and gaining the support of his frontline staff, something still bothered him. It felt like the impact of his business on the overall healthcare system was limited, and that without significantly more capital and resources, that was unlikely to change. He needed to find a way to scale up his endeavors. After Circle went public in 2011, he took the opportunity to step down and look for something else to do.

That something else was Babylon, a mobile healthcare app, designed to provide users with virtual consultations with doctors and healthcare professionals for a monthly fee. Remembering his own upbringing, Parsa was motivated to find a way to provide healthcare that could scale effectively to provide service not only to everyone in the UK but also other places in the world where citizens did not have access to adequate care.

Parsa's experience of running hospitals via Circle had taught him that 70 per cent of all the money that was spent on healthcare went into salaries. If he planned to serve more people by using doctors and nurses, he was not going to reduce costs enough to deliver a solution at scale.

"And remember, the $10 trillion we spend today in healthcare only serves half of the world population," Parsa explained to me, with an emphatic gesture. "Half of the world population has zero access to healthcare. Even if we had the money, there are not enough doctors. So there's got to be another solution. And the only other solution is what Google did with information. Google didn't go and set up libraries everywhere. Google created a free library for everybody."

In order to create a "free library" equivalent for healthcare, Babylon needed to find a way to leverage the expertise of human knowledge without hiring lots of humans. Parsa and his team began exploring ways of triaging patients and diagnosing conditions using algorithms and AI, while still relying on human doctors for more complex conditions and sensitive discussions. As they progressed, they realized that their model might have another major benefit in addition to being able to scale globally; it might also be a step toward addressing another key problem in healthcare: the diffusion of best practice.

"For human doctors, it takes seventeen years for best practice to become common practice," Parsa commented with a rueful shake of his head, "but a machine can do that instantaneously. When something's a best practice you just tell the machine and that's it."

What makes Ali Parsa an effective algorithmic leader is not just his company's use of AI, but also his ability to constantly reframe his objective—the global delivery of affordable healthcare—through the lens of technologies and practices that scale up.

Preserve your talent patterns

The importance of designing work is not all about finding new, innovative ways of doing things. Sometimes it can be just as important to preserve the knowledge you already have.

Every year, a significant number of the most valuable people in your organization will leave. Some will get better offers from rival firms, some will shift careers and find new things to do, and others will simply retire. In the United States alone, an estimated 10,000 Baby Boomers retire every day, taking with them all the institutional and human knowledge they have accumulated over a thirty- to forty-year career. This knowledge about how things work and how to get things done is the nuanced, contextual knowledge that doesn't live in spreadsheets, databases, or PDFs but rather inside human brains. I think of them as *talent patterns*.

Ganesh Padmanabhan is a VP at CognitiveScale, an AI startup in the field of augmented intelligence. Previously, Padmanabhan had launched a venture focused on explainable AI, as he had been fascinated by the problem of explainability. How do you explain a decision an AI made in the context of the user who needs to rely on that decision?

The venture didn't take off, but it landed Padmanabhan at CognitiveScale, where he started working on the related problem of empowering humans with systems that could learn and improve with time. For Padmanabhan, this was an important point of differentiation over more basic forms of algorithmic systems, like robotic process automation.

Robotic process automation, which essentially replaces a human operator with an algorithm that replicates their activities on a computer terminal, is a rules-based system. It takes a routine task that a human normally performs, whether it be filing documents or completing forms, and automates it. However, the moment you want to go a bit further and have the system deal with a more complex issue or a cognitive decision-making process, then the automated system hits a wall. Whatever the automated system has been programmed to do, it will continue to do in exactly the same way, whether it has done so ten times, a hundred times, or a million times. It will not and cannot deviate from that.

"The idea behind augmented intelligence is different," Padmanabhan explained to me, as he gestured at the teams of programmers visible through the glass walls of our meeting room. "Augmented intelligence is when you try to mimic human cognitive functions with a feedback loop in it. With a human in the picture, when you're surfacing a particular pattern and say, 'Here's a decision I recommend you make for this particular process,' you're giving them both reasons and the evidence for a recommendation. The human can then use their judgment and either agree or disagree, based on their intuition or experience."

"So, the system learns over time that the output is essentially one that shouldn't be weighted?" I asked.

"Exactly," said Padmanabhan. "The human being in the loop will also ensure the system is trained and gets better as you iterate through it. That is what makes augmented intelligence different from regular AI approaches."

Padmanabhan's vision of the human in the loop becomes even more important when you stop worrying about algorithms taking away human jobs and start imagining how you might preserve the patterns of knowledge that leak from organizations. What makes for a great customer experience, a positive interaction in a call center, or a caring moment in a medical facility relies on uniquely human patterns that are hard for machines to grasp, or evaluate, without our assistance.

Padmanabhan gave me the example of capturing the patterns of care managers who provide care for cancer patients, so that when a new hire comes in, they are prompted by a recommendation system that says, "These are the right steps to take because Joe Smith did this for thirty years, and he believed it was the best way to actually address this particular function."

You don't have to wait until the end of someone's career to preserve their talent pattern. Rather than simply automating obvious processes, algorithmic leaders should attempt to identity, record, and replicate the best behavioral patterns across their organization. In a data-driven organization, you can constantly iterate and test, and by doing so, gradually build a picture of what the ideal state of your organization or process should look like. By capturing the best in what people do, you can design a better organization.

Let your team own the work

Who owns the work? may seem like an odd question to ask, but in many large companies, there is a division between the technologists responsible for building applications, collecting data, and automating processes and the people who are responsible for making decisions, solving problems, and getting things done.

As a result, too much work gets done outside of the system. People download data from the company server and put it in a spreadsheet, which they then email around as an attachment. Team members make edits and save their own versions. Others print it out, scribble on it, and adorn it with sticky notes. The original author of the document organizes a meeting to discuss the project and creates an obnoxiously large PowerPoint deck to torture everyone with. Not that anyone is paying attention. All the project members bring their own version of the document to the meeting, and there is an argument about which version is the most up to date. Chaos ensues.

The spreadsheet as a fixture of executive life is a recent phenomenon. There were once entire rooms full of human bookkeepers who crunched company data in tabs and rows. But now that we work with real-time data and adaptive algorithms, we need new, more sophisticated tools. Basically, your team needs the ability to track, share, and automate processes in a way that they can adapt themselves, as your business and data change, without relying on your technology department to keep pace.

"There was a big movement in software development five or ten years ago for Agile software development," explained Rick Willett to me, as I sat down to interview him. "But in fact, I believe that no-code is the most agile form of software development. Instead of an iterative process of development teams talking to clients, doing two-week scrums, no-code blows that up. The client is effectively building the software."

The idea of letting employees, an IT department's clients, create their own applications, which can use and modify company data, may sound like insanity to those with traditional technology backgrounds. The vast majority of your employees will lack the ability to program. They are capable, however, of bringing their unique insight and judgment to designing smarter ways to work.

Willett is the CEO of Quick Base, a platform for allowing non-technical employees to build their own applications. Quick Base is a tool for manipulating and processing data from cloud platforms. Rather than spending days—or even months—doing manual data entry and moving content between spreadsheets, team members can design and modify processes using live information.

Willett, who started his career at GE, saw firsthand the perils of bureaucratic organizations and the disconnect that occurs as companies grow and management layers start to hoard and hide information. For Willett, giving employees the platforms they need to build their own software and automate processes—making them citizen developers—is also a way of breaking down the layers and hierarchies that plague traditional organizations.

Encouraging and empowering your team to be citizen developers is a step toward designing work, but tools alone are not enough. One of the biggest things holding back citizen development from wider adoption is the need to bridge the gap between flexibility and governance.

Business builders are not application builders. They don't automatically understand IT concepts of access controls, security, and testing. As you empower your team to design work, you also have to provide training around the sensitivity of data and on how to responsibly handle and manage what may become mission-critical applications.

Build a digital twin

Whereas many teenage boys growing up in the 1980s had a picture of a Lamborghini Countach on their walls, I idolized something a little different: the SR-71 Blackbird. It was like a piece of alien engineering (and some maintain that is exactly what it was). Wafer-thin at the edges, it is still the fastest air-breathing manned aircraft ever built, capable of taking you from New York to LA in just over an hour, and as high as 85,000 feet, right at the edge of space. The crazy part of the Blackbird story is that the plane was designed in the 1950s using pen and paper, without the aid of computers or sophisticated algorithms.

If the Blackbird was the pinnacle of analogue human brilliance, then its digital equivalent, while perhaps less immediately striking, is the conventional digital jet engine. The Rolls-Royce Trent engine is fitted to a wide variety of aircraft from the Airbus A330 to the Boeing 787 Dreamliner. It used to be that as an airliner's engine approached its end-of-life, the airline would buy a replacement engine, install it, and maintain it. The problem was, with many different kinds of planes in their fleet, often with multiple engine models to keep track of, the airline service departments were not doing a particularly good job of maximizing the life of their engines. They would either replace them too early or let them run too long, often until they failed spectacularly.

Rolls-Royce therefore developed a new subscription model that let the airlines buy power by the hour. For a flat hourly rate per engine, Rolls-Royce would handle everything from installation to maintenance. The new business model was transformative, both for the airlines, which could now reduce the complexity of their operations, and for Rolls-Royce, which now had a predictable, recurrent revenue model. But there was a problem. In order to make the transition, Rolls-Royce had to stop just making engines and start collecting data about engines as well.

Rolls-Royce started filling its engines with sensors that provided real-time data analytics about their performance. Even if a plane was mid-flight, data could be sent to an R&D center to be analyzed and then acted upon if necessary. Now that it was managing hundreds of thousands of engines, Rolls-Royce could also start to study the digital performance of its products at scale: understanding and predicting failure, discovering what types of maintenance were effective, and uncovering new ways to optimize fuel consumption. By designing and managing the digital version of its physical product, Rolls-Royce was able to transform itself from a manufacturer that competed with other vendors on price to an algorithmic partner to the airlines that was integral to their operating efficiently.

The Rolls-Royce Trent engine is an early example of a *digital twin*. A digital twin is a digital model of a physical object or process that allows you to optimize its performance. You could build a digital twin of a manufacturing line or a factory, a self-driving car, or even just a small component in a larger system, for example. With the right sensors and data, you could even create a digital twin of a shipping facility, a wind farm, or an organizational department. And just like the Trent engine, a digital twin is able to continually learn and update itself using data from its sensors. This ability allows you to run simulations, predict outcomes, and explore complex scenarios.

The final step in "designing work" rather than "doing work" is thinking about the digital version of what you do. By stepping back and conceiving of either your product or your overall process as something that can be abstracted, monitored, and configured virtually, you will discover not only opportunities for automation but also entirely new business models.

As the economist W. Brian Arthur argues, as company processes and products become more digital and modular, leaders will be able to access a library of existing virtual structures that they can use like LEGO pieces to build entirely new organizational models.

Machine intelligence may assist us with data gathering, analysis, and simulation, but it is ultimately up to us, as algorithmic leaders, to explore and design smarter ways of using those outputs.

SUMMARY

1 The real job of an algorithmic leader is not to work but to design work. The question you should be asking is not *Are we getting results?* but *Do we have the right approach?*

2 Look for the scaled-up solution. The story of Ali Parsa and Babylon Health illustrates not only how AI can disrupt a traditional industry, but also its role in building a service with global scale.

3 The importance of designing work is not limited to finding innovative ways of doing things; it includes identifying, preserving, and replicating talent patterns, or the implicit knowledge and expertise of your best people before they leave or retire.

4 Empowering your teams to be citizen developers ensures that the people closest to the work can have the biggest say in designing it. Employees should be able to design work, even if they lack formal programming skills.

5 A great example of using algorithms to design work is building a digital twin, or a digital version of your product, part, or process. In doing so, you may discover not only opportunities for automation but also entirely new business models.

QUESTION

If you could start your business again with a clean sheet of paper and the ability to leverage AI, algorithms, and automation, what would you do differently?

7

AUTOMATE AND ELEVATE

"Man is the lowest-cost, 150-pound,
nonlinear, all-purpose computer system which can
be mass-produced by unskilled labor."
NASA, 1965

Find the new job inside the old one

It will be impossible to think about productivity in the next few years without considering the impact of automation. You can safely assume that if something can be automated, it will be—if not by you, then almost certainly by one of your competitors.

The issue for algorithmic leaders, then, is not automation but what comes after. Does your new army of robotic resources finally give you the opportunity to streamline to the hilt by decimating your workforce?

The word "decimate" comes from the Latin *decemare* and literally means "to kill one of every ten." In Roman times, it was considered a pragmatic punishment approach for serious crimes committed within a large group. Apparently, the group that were to be punished would be divided into clusters of ten and made to draw lots. The person that lost the draw was executed by his nine companions, often by stoning or clubbing.

Rather than wondering if your job will disappear, ask yourself, *What is the new job inside my old one?* And as a leader, *Do I decimate or elevate the people around me?*

The question of whether automation should lead to decimation or elevation will soon become more relevant, as companies start applying algorithms and machine learning to activities previously performed by people. Automation has already led to the complete replacement of some roles, like elevator operators. Typically, however, partial automation of a job can actually lead to more of those jobs being created, especially if there is unmet demand for that product or service.

James Bessen, an economist and lecturer at the Boston University School of Law, studies the relationship between automation and employment. In Bessen's view, the key question is how technology boosts productivity—that is, how the economy produces goods and services in the most efficient way possible. Given that both capital and human labor are finite resources, doing more with less should translate into lower prices. And, as prices fall and more people can afford to buy more things, the market will expand such that companies will need to hire more people to meet the new demand.

History seems to support Bessen's theory. During the Industrial Revolution, for example, when automation was introduced to the cotton industry, weavers on power looms were suddenly able to produce 2.5 times the amount of coarse cloth per hour a weaver on a hand loom could. Later, improved technology would generate another twentyfold increase in output per hour. As the amount of human labor per yard of cloth fell, cloth became cheaper and people bought more, which increased demand. This resulted in the number of weavers in the United States quadrupling between 1830 and 1900 rather than falling.

Bessen discovered that a similar thing happened when ATMs were introduced into the banking industry. Everyone assumed that the automated teller machines would, almost by definition, eliminate human bank tellers and certainly, some tellers did lose their jobs. In the early 1990s, when ATMs started being introduced at scale, the average bank branch in an urban area required about twenty-one tellers. With the introduction of ATMs, this was cut to about thirteen tellers. However, now that it was cheaper to open branches, banks started opening up many more in convenient areas to serve customers, and as a platform for branding and marketing.

Once again, the demand for bank tellers increased, but their job had changed. It was no longer about counting money all day and doing routine, transactional tasks that could be either automated or replaced by customer self-service. It was now about building relationships with customers, cross-selling additional products, and performing other tasks that involved soft skills like human engagement, empathy, and judgment.

I was curious about how Bessen came to be so interested not only in the impact of automation on employment, but also in his other area of focus, patent innovation. Bessen explained that prior to becoming an academic, he had developed the first WYSIWYG desktop publishing program at a community newspaper in Philadelphia in 1983. That experience gave him a unique perspective on the impact of technology on the typesetting profession.

"Originally it was typesetters that controlled the publishing industry," he said, when I asked him about his own journey. "Theirs was a highly skilled craft. In the US, I think it was a four-year apprenticeship. It was something that required lots of skill, but it was also limited to just preparing the type. Then, we had desktop publishing and graphic design software like Photoshop. Suddenly a whole new set of skills were required. Some people made a nice transition. The people who had worked on the typesetting machines were able to become graphic designers. But there were also other cases where typesetters had difficulty making the transition. Particularly in the newspaper industry, there were some very dramatic changes, such as in Britain with Rupert Murdoch, where bitter strikes surrounded the implementation of the automated technology."

In Bessen's view, a stable and sustainable increase in jobs following automation depends on demand, on whether people's skills are complementary to the technology, and on the labor market institutions and how they develop. The impact of automation is rarely as simple as machines replacing humans. Generally it is humans with the ability to leverage technology replacing other humans, argues Bessen.

Some workers use AI in order to render their colleagues redundant. This actually speaks to the value of education and training, as the upgrading of employee skills in the algorithmic age is more of a strategic and economic necessity, rather than an employee benefit.

"My kids are graphic designers," continued Bessen as we were wrapping up our discussion. "This will be tough, even for them. There's still huge turmoil and change going on, and it's very hard for many designers to keep up with the technology. Many designers get trained in print design, and now there's Web design, mobile design, and other new formats. It seems to me the same sort of dynamic will play out as we have seen before. It's going to make certain sorts of skills more valuable and degrade other sorts of skills. As long as there's enough of the former, we should be okay."

Finding the new job inside the old one requires leaders to look beyond the scope of the original activity or process to figure out where value can really be created.

Manish Singh, an EVP at Oversight Systems (a technology company that uses AI to help companies with compliance and operations analysis), gave me an interesting example of how clerical work in finance departments is changing in the algorithmic age.

Large companies generally have entire teams of people focused on auditing expenditures such as corporate travel expenses. The job generally involves looking at one report at a time to see if there is any kind of policy violation or error, or even if the policy itself is problematic. With machine learning and AI, software can now automate a lot of that work. Rather than simply being checked for mistakes, the claim can be analyzed against not only all the claims that one particular employee might have submitted in the past but also all the claims made by other employees in similar circumstances. The point of this multidimensional analysis is not just to approve or deny an expense claim, but to gather evidence to support suspicions that there is a pattern, if necessary, and ultimately generate a recommendation. So, for example, if someone purchases some jewelry on their corporate card and classifies it on their expense claim form as a hotel stay, and they have done so three times in the last year, the AI-enabled system can identify this as a behavioral pattern that requires immediate action.

Automation from this perspective allows people to gain a new perspective in ways that would not have been feasible at that level of scale in the past. The role of the people working in the finance department can now be elevated from auditing and reconciling transactions to being strategic, mitigating risk, and changing behavior. Once a pattern has been identified, it is possible for someone to have a conversation with the employee concerned and change their behavior, rather than trying to catch problems one transaction at a time.

The idea is that if companies can de-risk their business process by automating risk mitigation via AI, then they can remove unnecessary manual steps such as manager approval for every expense and the requirement to reconcile every transaction. In essence, by de-risking the business process, they can automate more of the business process, create a better experience for everyone, and allow employees to do more interesting work.

Retrain, reequip, and reenergize

Automation might not entirely eliminate traditional jobs from your company, but it will absolutely change the nature of those jobs and the skills required to do them.

Imagine that you have a job as a retail merchandiser at Coca-Cola, and that you are responsible for visiting stores and kiosks, advising merchants on how to arrange their products, and checking compliance with the brand guidelines. Now, using a platform like Einstein by Salesforce, a customer can just take a picture of their store's fridge and the algorithm will tell them what to do and where to place their product. What will the purpose of the retail merchandiser be now that their job has been changed by AI? Which of their skills are still relevant, and what might a career migration path look like?

The rise of mass automation brings with it unavoidable, but not unaddressable, political and social consequences. We have been here before. Economist David Autor argues that near the end of the nineteenth century, agricultural states in America faced the prospect of mass unemployment as more automation was introduced into the farming industry. Rather than waiting to see what might happen, those states drove the high school movement, which required everyone to stay in school until the age of sixteen and became the basis for the K–12 education system that is still in place today.

That education system, however, may not be up to the task that we now face. Andrew Ng, also a pioneer in online education and co-founder of Coursera, believes that our challenge is to find a way to teach people to do non-routine, non-repetitive work. To date, our education system has not been good at doing that either at scale or fast enough to keep pace with rapid industry change.

That leaves a lot of the responsibility for education in the hands of employers. Some have already stepped up to the challenge. United Technologies, for example, pays employees' tuition bills up to $12,000 a year. Facebook offers free AI classes for all their employees, whether or not they work in IT, while Microsoft's performance review system includes an appraisal of how employees have learned from others and how they have applied that knowledge.

However, training is not enough, unless it helps employees migrate to a new way of working and thinking. A good example of a scaled-up migration initiative is AT&T's Workforce Reskilling and Pivot Program. AT&T is one of the world's largest employers. The average tenure at AT&T is twelve years, twenty-two if you don't count the people working in call centers. Internal research completed in 2013 found that 100,000 of AT&T's 240,000 workers were in roles that the company probably wouldn't need in a decade. Worse, when the company's leadership began to analyze the kinds of roles that they would need, they realized there were serious skill gaps. The company would need a lot more coding skills, for example, and more leaders who could make smart decisions based on data and analytics.

To address this, the company kicked off a major reorganization. They streamlined the thousands of job titles that existed at AT&T into fewer and broader categories that clustered similar skills. This simpler classification allowed employees to start planning a more diverse career path through the company and to focus on the new skills they would need.

As part of this overhaul, AT&T created an online system called Career Intelligence that allowed their employees to identify alternative positions, see what skills were required, find out how many positions are available, investigate whether the segment was projected to grow or shrink, and explore what they might earn. However, there was a catch: while the training was free and some of the learning modules could be done at work, employees would have to do much of the work on their own time.

The challenge for companies building retraining programs is that AI is evolving so rapidly, it will be hard to pin down the skills and capabilities that people will need. Even worse than not training an employee for a future job is training them for a job that no longer exists by the time they are ready. Workers will need to constantly upgrade themselves as machines evolve. Algorithmic leaders will have a responsibility, and an incentive, to ensure that both they and the people around them are able to stay just a little further ahead on the curve of the AI revolution in order to remain relevant and valuable.

While lifelong learning is a standard cliché of large organizations, it takes on an entirely new meaning in an age of machine intelligence.

Create a team to rethink teams

Another way of elevating, or upgrading, the people who work around you is to create teams to rethink teams.

The primary function of these meta-teams is to support and augment a traditional business function with data, algorithms, and other forms of technological infrastructure. Typically, these teams have the word "operations" in their title. So, for example, a marketing operations team will support the marketing function by collecting and analyzing customer data, maintaining marketing automation platforms, and designing digital workflows around communications and content.

Similarly, you might have an HR operations team that collects data on the workforce and manages reporting and analytics across diverse teams and departments, as well as looking for opportunities to leverage technology to automate activities like onboarding, internal transfers, or leaves of absence. Amazon, for example, has a team handling these kinds of activities that they call Global HR Operations and Analytics.

A good operations team is not just focused on operational efficiency and automating processes, it also plays an active role in reimagining the function that it is supporting. A good example of this is how Google runs its legal team.

Mary O'Carroll is the head of Legal Operations at Google, which has one of the world's largest and most active internal legal departments of any organization, with about 1,000 people dispersed across the planet. They have to deal with everything from requests for confidential information to patent applications, and complex tax structures to the regulatory implications of cutting-edge technologies.

"You have probably heard the saying, 'Make sure we run Legal like a business.' The Legal department, unlike most functions in the corporate world like HR, IT, or Finance, has not had the same level of scrutiny on efficiency, budgets, or value for money," explained O'Carroll when I had the chance to ask her about the rationale for setting up the Legal Operations team at Google.

"Legal Operations was created to focus on managing our financial relationships (our technology vendors and law firms), all of our systems and tools that we have in-house, and what I call strategy. Strategy concerns internal operations. We are responsible for making sure the trains are running on time as well as looking at our processes and making sure that they are optimized for quality, speed, and cost."

Given that this is Google, a big part of O'Carroll and her team's job is looking for ways to leverage technology, data, and algorithms to increase the access to legal knowledge in the firm without having to hire many more lawyers. For example, they have deployed self-service tools based on decision trees to help internal clients get the answers that they need. These tools either remove the need for a lawyer completely or facilitate the collection of the necessary data that a lawyer is likely to need to help them on a particular issue.

The Legal Operations team also uses contract analytics and machine learning to pull out metadata and clauses from contracts that would otherwise require a lot of reading. Machine learning is used to automatically tag attributes of patents so that Google employees can quickly look at entire portfolios without a lot of manual work being done by humans.

When I asked her about whether this might ultimately lead to fewer lawyers being employed at Google, O'Carroll replied, "That's not our goal. We're eliminating some of the low-valued work that is currently very manual. We are focused on automating work that people don't want to do."

In fact, just as eDiscovery software has affected the legal profession (see the Introduction), the increased accessibility of professional advice through automation at Google may actually be increasing the overall demand for legal services at the firm.

One of the most important initiatives that O'Carroll kicked off when she joined Google was a data-driven dashboard to manage their outside law firms. They extract all the data from their electronic billing systems to show spending by region, with analytics around how much the spending differs from the budgets. For O'Carroll, the dashboard is a platform for transparency. Her general counsel is always asking her questions like *Are we getting good value for money? How much are we spending on average, on discovery? How much do we spend to get to this certain phase of a patent? How much do we spend in this country or with this law firm?*

With the dashboard, she not only has the answer to such questions at her fingertips, she also has a useful drill-down capacity to probe deeper. For example, once they know what their total billings are, her team is able to have an informed discussion with providers about the nature of their activities. They can delve down into what is driving their billings, which particular matters are involved, how many people are on the case, and the seniority of the people assigned to their team.

I was interested to learn that the scope of the Legal Operations team at Google extends beyond elevating the lawyers that work there to driving change more broadly in the industry. In O'Carroll's view, one of the best ways to disrupt the legal industry is through standardization. In many ways, the legal industry has been relatively resistant to change. Every company does things differently, which means that law firms also customize their solutions, contracts, and advice in infinitely different ways.

In addition to her role at Google, O'Carroll is on the leadership team of the Corporate Legal Operations Consortium (CLOC). When members of this group started talking to each other, they realized that the traditional level of customization was often unnecessary. They had the same goals and only came up with different approaches because there was no standard playbook for getting things done. Standardization, for CLOC and Google, is one of the ways in which they plan to challenge the highly bespoke nature of legal services today.

In O'Carroll's view, lawyers are knowledge workers. They want to work on interesting, high-value activities, rather than reinventing the wheel—and their clients want this experience for them as well. She encourages her legal partners to design smarter knowledge management, and collaboration systems, to automate routine activities, with the ultimate goal of elevating the role and value of lawyers.

Reimagine, don't just replace work

Automation is not only an opportunity to elevate your teams; it is also an invitation to profoundly reimagine what you do.

Challenge yourself to look beyond the obvious. What things can you do now that you simply couldn't do before? What are the new approaches to solving problems and creating products that would not be possible without smarter algorithms?

Let's look at Goldman Sachs. You might imagine that taking a job at Goldman Sachs would mean joining an exclusive and conservative world of Wall Street investment banking: trading and underwriting securities, advising on deals, and taking companies public. Perhaps that was true in the past, but things are changing because of the possibilities offered by automation and algorithms.

Before the financial crash of 2007, the US cash equities trading desk at Goldman Sachs's New York headquarters employed 600 traders. Today there are just two. (When I mentioned that number to Manoj Narang, the hedge fund manager we met earlier in this book, he was openly surprised there were even that many.) Suddenly, with those 600 traders gone, there were a lot of empty desks. So Goldman decided to use that available real estate to house small groups of internal technology startups created to leverage data and machine learning.

An interesting example of one of those startups is Marcus, a retail bank named after the founder of Goldman Sachs. Marcus was initially created to help consumers consolidate their credit card balances. It is entirely run by software, with no human intervention, and was launched in under a year. In its first eighteen months of operation, it issued $3 billion in new consumer loans. The interesting part of the story is that companies like Marcus, designed to operate mainly with automation and algorithms, have allowed Goldman Sachs to move into consumer finance, something that was previously quite unthinkable given its focus on investment banking.

You can find similar examples across a wide range of industries. Automation is not just about cutting costs. It has also led to radical new approaches to creating products. Nike, for example, did not merely automate the die cutters and hydraulic presses that it traditionally uses to make shoes. It partnered with Flex, a technology company that makes consumer electronic goods like Fitbits.

When Flex first got the contract with Nike, it ordered fifty different pairs of shoes online with the intention of taking them apart and seeing how they were made. The inspiration for this act of vandalism came from Nike's own history. Nike's co-founder Bill Bowerman, a track-and-field coach, had begun making running shoes by literally disassembling existing ones with a saw, investigating their insides, and looking for unnecessary elements to remove. By saving ounces from shoes, he could save seconds from an athlete's performance times. Now, Nike was trying to save the wait time for custom shoes. To keep up with the demands for personalization, it wanted to reduce the production time for a single unique shoe from weeks to days.

Traditional shoe production requires a lot of materials and labor. There can be as many as 200 different pieces across ten sizes, often cut and glued together by hand. Flex, an outsider to the shoe industry, brought a fresh approach. It introduced two ideas previously considered to be impossible: the automated gluing of materials and the use of lasers to cut materials. The engineers at Flex, accustomed to solving supply chain problems on complex electronic goods, invented a process whereby any material, soft or hard, could be laser-cut into whatever pattern was needed, right on the factory floor. Rather than being created from a sewing pattern, the Nike shoe was now produced on demand via a digital file.

Whether it be entering a new market or working with new partners, automation is an opportunity to reimagine and elevate what you do.

Focus on the exceptions

If you can automate the routine, predictable parts of a leader's job, how should a leader then spend their time? What is the best use of a leader's cognitive surplus? In short: managing exceptions.

Hyderabad in the south of India is a rapidly developing IT hub. When I was on a speaking tour there, someone showed me a picture of the operations center of a large Australian bank that was located there. The company had just implemented robotic process automation. To avoid alarming their employees, the bank had set up computer terminals and desks for their new algorithms, with the label "robot" above each one. In a rare example of workers responding well to automation, the employees at the operations center were so impressed with the diligence and efficiency of their new digital co-workers that they voted to give them the best desks in the office, by the windows.

In the next few years, robotic process automation software will take over much of the administrative and clerical work normally done by people. This form of automation replaces routine business processes by mimicking the way that people interact with applications through a standard user interface and following simple rules to make decisions. You will see this kind of technology used to automate processes like the onboarding of new employees or customers, managing accounts payable, processing of invoices, and managing compliance and risk management activities.

Process automation presents a big problem for traditional global service centers like the one I saw in Hyderabad. Even low-cost workers can't compete with the efficiency and scale of low-cost algorithms, unless they rethink the value that they can bring. Humans are vital resources, even in a highly automated back-office, but their role has to shift from working cheaply to doing things that rule-based machines can't do—namely, handling exceptions to the rules. And doing so quickly.

Speed is of the essence. As platforms get better at identifying when a problem exists, human leaders have to be more proactive at responding to avert a crisis or seize an opportunity. As Martin Dewhurst and Paul Willmott from McKinsey & Company argue in their report *Manager and Machine: The New Leadership Equation*, although executives can spend less time on day-to-day management issues, when the exception report signals a difficulty, the ability to spring into action will help executives differentiate themselves and the health of their organizations from their competitors (human or otherwise).

Exceptions, in their view, come in two forms: those that require insight, such as knowing when to intervene (setting new credit limits for a big customer, for example), and those that require inspiration (galvanizing the organization to respond quickly, work in new ways, or do something innovative, for example).

Part of knowing the best way to elevate the people on our teams is knowing our strengths and limitations. As humans, while we are conditioned to seek out patterns, we struggle to do so when presented with large amounts of data. We also suffer from cognitive noise, which leads us to be unreliable, or at least inconsistent, when making highly repetitive, similar decisions. We do, however, possess the ability to resolve divergent trends and find "new choices" in ways that you might call nonlinear, intuitive, or emergent.

All of this is good news for our future. You don't need to look too far if you want to automate and elevate. Humans, it turns out, can excel at managing exceptions and understanding the context of a problem, especially when there is a scarcity of data, significant ambiguity, or numerous contradictions in what is known or provided.

SUMMARY

1 Rather than simply eliminating jobs, automation changes them. The important question to ask yourself is not *When will my job disappear?* but *What is the new job inside my old one?*

2 As jobs transform, new skills will be required. Algorithmic leaders need to invest in their own capabilities to stay ahead of the AI revolution, and to remain relevant and valuable.

3 As illustrated by the story of the Google Legal Operations team, one effective way to elevate people is to create a team to rethink teams. A good operations team not only exists to gain greater efficiency but also seeks to constantly reinvent the function itself.

4 Automation is not only an opportunity to elevate your teams; it is also an invitation to profoundly reimagine what you do. Challenge yourself to explore things that you can do now but couldn't do before the age of algorithms.

5 As we start automating more of the repetitive parts of daily work, the most valuable use of your time will be managing exceptions and finding nonlinear solutions to complex problems.

QUESTION

In the next five years, what roles or activities within roles will no longer exist in your team, and what new skills or capabilities will be the most in demand?

PART III

CHANGE
THE
WORLD

8

IF THE ANSWER IS X, ASK Y

"When an online service is free, you're not the customer. You're the product."
TIM COOK, CEO OF APPLE

Pick the right moral compass

One of your most important responsibilities in the algorithmic age is to ask *Why*? If the algorithm says the answer is X, why is it X?

Why did the algorithm make that prediction? Why did we optimize for those outcomes? Why did we handle our customer data in this way? Why did our legal team make our user agreement twenty pages long?

As you may have noticed, these questions are tough because they deal with ethics and values. In order to get meaningful answers, you will need to face some complex moral dilemmas. What exactly should your moral compass be? Is it enough to comply with the law, or do you need an alternative benchmark for right and wrong?

It's challenging to navigate ethics in the digital age. As a leader in the twenty-first century, you will face difficult choices, and so will your organization. Your customers will expect you to use their data to create personalized and anticipatory services for them while demanding that you prevent the inappropriate use and manipulation of their information. Hackers, terrorists, and rogue states will influence the agenda by raising the digital threat level. Regulators, politicians, and other government authorities will seek to define and protect their own position as public awareness grows.

Given all these challenges, Google's former unofficial motto, "Don't be evil," seems both prescient and naive. As we create systems that are more capable of understanding and targeting services at individual users, our capacity to do evil will grow exponentially. And yet, this also raises the question of what exactly is evil? Is it breaking the law, breaking your industry code of conduct, or breaking user trust?

In 2013, researchers Michal Kosinski, David Stillwell, and Thore Graepel published an academic paper in the *Proceedings of the National Academy of Sciences* that became a useful case study for examining ethics in an algorithmic age and set the stage for what would become a watershed moment for digital privacy.

Titled "Private Traits and Attributes Are Predictable from Digital Records of Human Behavior," the paper demonstrated that Facebook "Likes" (which were publicly open by default at that time) could be used to automatically and accurately predict a range of highly sensitive personal attributes, including sexual orientation and gender, ethnicity, religious and political views, personality traits, use of addictive substances, parental separation status, and age. High intelligence, for example, could be predicted from a user's feelings about thunderstorms and curly fries; strong indicators of low intelligence included a liking for Sephora and Harley-Davidson.

What was particularly striking was the researchers' discovery that while people could choose not to reveal certain pieces of information about their lives, such as their sexual orientation or political preferences, this information could still be predicted in a statistical sense from aspects of their lives that they did reveal. That was important, because few users were associated with Likes that explicitly revealed their attributes. For example, less than 5 per cent of users identified as gay were connected with explicitly gay groups. Similarly, your willingness to support the ideas of the Democrats might be more accurately predicted by whether you liked Hello Kitty than whether you liked Barack Obama.

When they published their study, the researchers acknowledged that their findings risked being misused by third parties to incite discrimination, for example. However, where others saw danger and risk, Aleksandr Kogan, one of Kosinski's colleagues at Cambridge University, saw opportunity. In early 2014, Cambridge Analytica, a British political consulting firm, signed a deal with Kogan for a private venture that would capitalize on the work of Kosinski and his team.

Soon after, Kogan created a personality quiz called thisisyour digitallife; Cambridge Analytica then paid for people to take it. As with many popular quizzes in lifestyle magazines, the app prompted users to answer questions in return for a psychological profile. In order to take the test, the user had to have a Facebook account and be a registered US voter so that the profiles could be matched to electoral records. The app then combined the results of each quiz with data not only from the user's Facebook account but also from their Facebook friends' accounts.

Kogan was able to create the quiz because of an initiative at Facebook that allowed third parties to access user data. A few years earlier, in April 2010, Facebook had created a platform called Open Graph, which allowed external developers to communicate with Facebook users and request permission to access their personal data—and, importantly for this story, to access their friends' data as well. Almost 300,000 users were estimated to have taken the test. It later emerged that Cambridge Analytica then exploited the data it had harvested via the test to access and build profiles on 87 million Facebook users.

It wasn't the first time that social media had been used in the context of US politics. Initially, Facebook was used by political parties as a tool for coordinating grassroots supporters. Chris Hughes, a co-founder of Facebook, left the company in early 2007 to work for then-Senator Barack Obama's new-media campaign. As part of that team, he led the development of My.BarackObama.com, a platform that attracted over 2 million volunteers, and helped to plan and market 200,000 offline events and raise over $30 million.

For their reelection campaign in 2012, Obama's team focused even more heavily on technology. They hired analysts, technologists, and digital marketing experts who had previously specialized in online retail and e-commerce. In the first election, Obama had six data analysts. The second time around, he had eighty. The new data team particularly favored A/B testing. A/B testing, the preferred tool of online retailers, is a data-driven way of determining the best of multiple options. Every time Obama's team sent out an email for funding or support, they would try multiple versions of subject lines, wording formats, and calls to action, and then adjust according to which performed the best within their database.

In late 2013, I found myself in Oslo sharing a taxi with Jim Messina, who had been the White House deputy chief of staff for operations under President Barack Obama from 2009 to 2011 and had served as the campaign manager for the 2012 reelection campaign. I asked him what he had learned from his experience.

Messina explained that in the planning phases of the campaign, he had met with a wide range of iconic leaders to try to work out what the formula for winning the election might be. Eric Schmidt, CEO of Google, warned him not to hire anyone from the world of politics, as they needed to try something entirely new. Anna Wintour, the editor of *Vogue*, told him to change the logo, because then all the supporters would need to buy the new T-shirts. Steven Spielberg told him that while winning the first time was like the Rolling Stones in the 1960s, this time around things would be different. Now that the rockers were older and more famous, and the concert tickets were expensive, engaging people would be harder. For Spielberg, that meant that they had to make the campaign sexy again.

Steve Jobs held up his iPhone and said, "If everything you do is not on this in sixteen months, you will lose." He explained that in 2008 it was all about their website, but this time it would be about what was happening everywhere else on the Web and on smartphones.

Interestingly, just like Cambridge Analytica, the Obama campaign would also create a Facebook app designed to extract user data. The app allowed supporters to donate, learn about voting requirements, and find nearby houses to canvass. The app asked users' permission to scan their photos, lists of friends, and news feeds. The key difference was that the people signing up for the service knew that the data they were handing over would be used to support a political campaign (although their friends did not). People who used the Cambridge Analytica–associated app had no idea that their data would be used to aid any political campaigns. That app was just described as a personality quiz that would be used by Cambridge University researchers.

The real game changer for Obama's campaign in 2012, however, was not Facebook, but the data from set-top boxes that had become recently available. Now the campaign could correlate voter preferences with TV show–watching preferences. Messina estimated that access to this data saved them over $40 million in buying efficiency and also uncovered new patterns that meant they could target a segment without buying prime time slots. Basically, the data showed them exactly which TV shows to buy, as they could correlate voting patterns with specific viewership segments.

I asked Messina how he thought that the technology war might escalate in the next election. He said that it would reach a point where you could effectively program your messaging and advertising to specific voters, and in a way, this would mean the end of democracy. Little did I know that even as we were having that conversation, forces were already in motion to make his comment alarmingly prophetic.

By 2014, Facebook had realized that it might have a problem on its hands and adapted its rules to limit third-party access to user data. The change meant that developers could not access a user's friends' data without obtaining their explicit permission. Cambridge Analytica, however, still had the data that it had harvested the year before. And by late 2015, the *Guardian* was reporting that Cambridge Analytica had been engaged to help Ted Cruz's presidential campaign get an edge over his Republican rival Donald Trump by using psychological data and profiling in a similar way to Kosinski and his team. In response to the story, Facebook sought to ban Kogan's app and get Cambridge Analytica to delete the data it had obtained.

By early 2016, right before the US presidential election, Trump's campaign team began investing heavily in Facebook ads, with Cambridge Analytica playing a crucial helping role. In mid-March 2018, whistleblower Christopher Wylie, who had worked at the firm, revealed to the *Guardian* and *New York Times* that his company had used Kogan's original data to develop voter profiles of people to deliver political messaging.

Facebook CEO Mark Zuckerberg was slow to respond to the growing public outcry. When he finally spoke out, he called it an "issue," a "mistake," and a "breach of trust," but tellingly, not a data breach. Two weeks later, Facebook took out full-page ads in the UK and US, once again apologizing for the "breach of trust" and admitting that the company could have done more to prevent data on millions of users being compromised.

By this time, regulators were starting to circle. The Federal Trade Commission announced there would be an investigation into whether the handling of Facebook user data violated a 2011 consent decree that had followed a two-year-long investigation by the agency into Facebook's privacy practices.

Was Facebook's mistake a twofold one of not setting the right policies for handling their user data up front and sharing that information too openly with their partners? Should they have anticipated the reaction of the US senators, who eventually called a Congressional hearing and spent more resources on lobby groups? Would a more comprehensive user agreement have shielded Facebook from liability? Or was this simply a case of bad luck? Was providing research data to Kogan a reasonable action to take at the time?

As an algorithmic leader, how would you have handled the choices confronting Facebook both before and during the crisis? One way of analyzing Facebook's decisions from an ethical standpoint is to look at a similar situation faced by Apple.

Over the last ten years, Apple has been criticized for taking the opposing stance on many issues relative to its peers like Facebook and Google. Unlike them, Apple runs a closed ecosystem with tight controls: you can't load software on an iPhone unless it has been authorized by Apple. The company was also one of the first to fully encrypt its devices, including deploying end-to-end encryption on iMessage and FaceTime for communication between users. When the FBI demanded a password to unlock a phone, Apple refused and went to court to defend its right to do so. Apple pioneered efforts to block iOS device advertising tracking by cookies. When it launched Apple Pay, it kept customer transactions private rather than recording all the data for its own analytics.

One key difference between Facebook and Apple is the agreement each has with their users. The Facebook user agreement is a complex legal document, constantly changing and difficult to understand. The Apple user agreement is simpler, which to me indicates a more customer-focused approach.

While Facebook's actions may have been within the letter of the law, and within the bounds of industry practice, at the time, they did not have the users' best interests at heart. This is what Zuckerberg ultimately meant when he said that Facebook had breached the trust of its users. There may be a simple reason for this. Apple sells products to consumers. At Facebook, the product is the consumer. Facebook sells consumers to advertisers.

While it is still early days for the great ethical AI debates that may define the next decade, one principle is apparent: You can't serve two masters. In the end, you either build a culture based on following the law or you focus on empowering users. The choice might seem to be an easy one, but it is more complex in practice.

Acting in the best interests of the customer goes beyond legal compliance; in the short term, it is unarguably more expensive. Your reward will be your customers' loyalty.

Avoid automating bias

When it comes to ethics, algorithmic leaders also need to be vigilant to the possibility of bias in the systems that they design and manage.

The idea that machines are somehow more impartial than humans and less susceptible to bias ignores the reality of their data and programming. Not only it is possible to create an algorithm that reflects the biases of the people who created it, but you can also inadvertently automate that bias at scale.

Machines can suffer from bias in the same way that people can, although our biases tend to be of a different nature. Human bias generally arises from our heuristics, or mental shortcuts, that we have evolved to make up for our shortfalls in thinking. For example, we jump to familiar conclusions when faced with decisions (availability bias), or place undue weight on our personal experiences (anchoring), or select evidence that supports our preconceived beliefs (confirmation bias).

Machine bias, however, arises from design, data, and automation. Is the most popular song on a website the one that everyone likes the most, or the first to reach number one in a top 10 list? The design of an algorithm can lead to confirmation bias. A machine learning algorithm can uncover previously unnoticed patterns in data, but if the data itself is flawed, or missing key attributes, then the predictive model that arises from that data will also be biased.

Caroline Sinders is a data ethnographer, a relatively new type of job for a world in which the culture of datasets is becoming as important as the design of interfaces. With a background in photojournalism as well as computer science, Sinders learned from photography the value of both observing people and thinking about the politics of images, framing, and representation.

When I spoke to her about what it takes to identify and avoid algorithmic bias, Sinders explained that the key issue is knowing the ingredients of your dataset. As we delegate more decisions to systems trained on data, understanding the components of those datasets is a concern not just for programmers but also for senior leaders throughout an organization.

Leaders need to know how to ask the right kinds of questions about their data. How old is the data, how big is the dataset, who assembled it, how diverse and representative is it? Was the data collected for a narrow, specific purpose or a more general one? While machine learning techniques are great at identifying statistical patterns, they can also leave out diverse, but potentially relevant outliers, as they aim to find the generalized case.

Early in her career, Sinders worked with Clay Shirky, a theorist on how people organize on the Web, which sparked an interest in designing for digital communities and natural language systems. That took her to IBM Watson, where she quickly realized that despite the wealth of engineering knowledge, there was a surprising lack of awareness around the cultural issues associated with data.

In Sinders's view, to properly create algorithmic systems, organizations have to be set up to ask the right kinds of questions. Designers have to be strategists who think deeply about people, engineers need to understand ethical choices, and leaders need to debate and discuss all the potential scenarios in which things could go wrong.

An important part of making this happen is ensuring that there is sufficient diversity in your organization to bring different viewpoints and perspectives to the process.

"I think that the major issue when it comes to creating accidental bias in systems is that there is a lack of diversity for someone to catch the faults they made or to ask the right questions," explained Sinders when we met.

Diversity is not only racial or cultural, it strongly relates to gender as well. The tech industry remains overwhelmingly dominated by men. LivePerson recently conducted a survey of US consumers in which they asked respondents if they could name a famous woman leader in tech. Only 8.3 per cent said they could; of those, a quarter named "Siri" or "Alexa" as their examples.

We are already seeing a growing number of cases where algorithms are struggling to adjust to the diversity of the world. The Google Photos machine learning algorithm identified black men as gorillas. The photo filter app FaceApp released a feature that was supposed to make users look "hot" but instead gave them features like lighter skin and rounder eyes. Microsoft's chatbot, Tay, was designed as an experiment to engage Millennials by learning to speak their own language from interacting with them on social platforms like Twitter. Within twenty-four hours, those very same eighteen- to twenty-year-olds had trained it to be so violent and racist that it had to be taken offline for "some adjustments."

Sometimes, algorithmic systems can further entrench not only stereotypes but also economic and social divides. ProPublica found in 2016, for example, that the software algorithms used to predict future criminals were heavily biased against black defendants. This came as no surprise to Kate Crawford, a principal researcher at Microsoft Research, as in her view, datasets reflect not only the culture but also the hierarchy of the world that they were made in. Algorithms can reinforce and amplify existing prejudices. For Crawford, the ultimate questions for fairness in machine learning are *Who is going to benefit from the system we are building?* and *Who might be harmed?*

Sometimes there are no good answers to such questions. Part of being an effective algorithmic leader is knowing when machine learning platforms are incapable of generating socially acceptable results. At that point, human-designed automated models may be the only option.

Tobias Baer, a partner in McKinsey & Company's Taipei office, and Vishnu Kamalnath, a specialist in the North American Knowledge Center in Massachusetts, argue that there are times when the best way to avoid bias is simply not to use machine learning algorithms. There is a trade-off to consider: algorithms offer speed and convenience, while manually crafted models such as decision trees, logistic regression, or even a human making a decision offer an approach that will provide more flexibility and transparency.

The key lesson for algorithmic leaders is to not just be aware of the possibility of bias, but to ensure you have a diverse enough team who can help you see more deeply into the implications of the systems that you build and help you craft alternatives where necessary.

Understand the explainability trade-off

One of the biggest sources of anxiety about AI is not that it will turn against us but that we simply cannot understand how it works.

Machine learning algorithms are sometimes called a black box, because they resemble a closed system that takes an input and produces an output, without any explanation as to why.

Knowing "why" is important for many industries, particularly those with fiduciary obligations like consumer finance, or in healthcare and education, where vulnerable lives are involved, or in military or government applications where you need to be able to justify your decisions.

Unfortunately, when it comes to deep learning platforms, explainability is problematic. If you could map a relationship simply enough between inputs and outputs to explain it, you probably wouldn't need machine learning in that context at all. The use of neural networks and adaptive algorithms means that in many cases, the AI is being programmed by AI itself. The resulting map of connections, while powerfully predictive, presents a problem when it comes to accountability.

In contrast to using a hand-coded system, you can't just look inside a neural network and see how it works. Not even the people who create complex AI systems can fully explain how or why they reach a particular conclusion. Like a human brain, a neural network is composed of thousands of simulated neurons, arranged in interconnected layers that each receive input and output signals that are then fed into the next layer, and so on until a final output is reached.

Deep Patient, for example, is a deep learning platform at Mount Sinai Hospital in New York. It was trained using electronic health records from 700,000 individuals and became adept at predicting disease, discovering patterns hidden in the hospital data that provided early warnings for patients at risk of developing a wide variety of ailments, including liver cancer, without human guidance.

Then, much to everyone's surprise, Deep Patient also demonstrated an ability to predict the onset of certain psychiatric disorders like schizophrenia, which are notoriously difficult even for doctors to predict. The challenge for medical professionals in such a scenario is to balance acknowledging the efficacy and value of the system with knowing how much to trust it, given that they don't fully understand it or how it works.

Some organizations and industries are investing in the capability to audit and explain machine learning systems. The Defense Advanced Research Projects Agency (DARPA) is currently funding a program called Explainable AI whose goal is to interpret the deep learning that powers drones and intelligence-mining operations. Capital One, a bank holding company, also created a research team dedicated to finding ways to make deep learning more explainable, as US regulations require this type of company to explain decisions such as why they denied a credit card to a prospective customer.

Algorithmic regulation is likely to be more sophisticated over the next few years, as the public starts to become more openly concerned about the impact of AI on their lives. For example, under the General Data Protection Regulation, which came into effect in 2018, the European Union requires companies to be able to explain a decision made by one of its algorithms.

The rationale behind algorithmic regulation is accountability. Making AI more explainable is not just about reassuring leaders that they can trust algorithmic decisions; it is also about providing a recourse for people to challenge AI-based decisions. In fact, the issue of algorithmic transparency applies not only to machine learning, but also to any algorithm whose inner workings are kept hidden.

Algorithms that either appear to be biased or are obscure in the way they work have already been challenged in the courts. For example, in 2014, the Houston Federation of Teachers brought a lawsuit against the Houston school district, arguing that the district's use of a secret algorithm to determine how teachers were evaluated, fired, and given bonuses was unfair. The system was developed by a private company, which classified its algorithm as a trade secret and refused to share it with teachers. Without knowing how they were being scored, teachers said, they were denied the right to challenge their terminations or evaluations. A circuit court found that the unexplainable software violated the teachers' 14th amendment rights to due process, and the case was ultimately settled in 2016, with use of the algorithm being discontinued. In the next few years, the number of such challenges is likely to rise.

One of the reasons that AI systems can be so effective is that they can offer solutions that by their very nature may not be immediately obvious to humans, so there may be good reasons for using such tools, even before they are completely explainable. The challenge for leaders is to identify the kinds of problems in their organization that are suitable for the application of algorithmic solutions—that generally means seeking AI-generated solutions to problems that are not controversial, or politically or socially sensitive.

Take data centers, for example. As data centers become larger and more powerful, they struggle increasingly with the sheer amount of heat that their servers generate. Such heating issues have led some companies to take extreme measures that have included, to date, Microsoft locating data centers under the ocean off the coast of Scotland and Facebook building an operations center in a remote, northern region of Sweden. As we discussed previously, DeepMind's approach—using AI to control the cooling of Google's data centers—was able to strike a balance between the potentially inexplicable actions recommended by the algorithm and a set of security protocols designed by human beings.

Even though in an ideal world we would prefer to fully comprehend the recommendations and predictions made by AI systems, the reality is that algorithmic leaders may instead need to find acceptable compromises, with appropriate safeguards, in order to stay competitive. In fact, rather than fully understanding how an AI thinks, it may be more useful to simply understand what the algorithms are optimized for.

Pick the right target

I'll be honest with you: I don't entirely trust car navigation apps.

One of my lingering suspicions when using an app like Waze or Google Maps to navigate to my destination is that rather than selecting the fastest route for me personally, it has calculated a slightly non-optimal route that optimizes congestion avoidance for everyone. Of course, I accept that there is a certain logic to a network being managed as a whole. The alternative would be anarchy. But secretly, I rather like the idea of having my own adversarial car AI that gets me to my destination faster than anyone else.

You can learn a lot about AI by knowing what it is optimized for. Focusing on optimization avoids crippling systems by demanding full explainability. Technology theorist David Weinberger, for example, argues that dumbing down deep learning platforms to the extent that we can actually understand them would undermine the reason we use algorithms in the first place: their complexity and nuance. Weinberger believes we should be more concerned with choosing an appropriate algorithmic target than with trying to understand how an algorithm came to specific conclusions.

Optimums are important. The classic thought experiment proposed by Swedish philosopher Nick Bostrom is called the Paperclip Maximizer. It describes how an AI could end up destroying the world. In a 2003 paper titled "Ethical Issues in Advanced Artificial Intelligence," Bostrom writes that "one way for it to happen is that a well-meaning team of programmers make a big mistake in designing its goal system. This could result, to return to the earlier example, in a superintelligence whose top goal is the manufacturing of paperclips, with the consequence that it starts transforming first all of earth and then increasing portions of space into paperclip manufacturing facilities."

The AI in Bostrom's paper is not intrinsically evil. It was simply, in his view, given the wrong goal and no constraints. Wrong goals or optimums can cause a lot of unintended harm. For example, an AI program that set school schedules in Boston was scrapped after an outcry from working parents and others who objected that it did not take into account their schedules and that it seemed to be focused on efficiency at the expense of education. But was it the program's fault? It was, after all, coded to look for ways to save money.

Some optimization debates are captured by the concept of trolley problems, philosophical thought experiments that date back fifty years to when people debated whether the driver of a runaway tram should veer into a wall to avoid hitting a pedestrian, and in doing so, potentially kill all of the passengers onboard. With the advent of self-driving cars, we once again have to consider the ethical considerations of allowing a vehicle to kill one person if, in doing so, it would save the lives of several people. Trolley problems present us with ethical paradoxes, but few practical frameworks to design algorithms or algorithmic societies.

Algorithms, like any system, are not perfect. AI is a tool that reflects our priorities, as organizations and governments. It might seem cold to discuss human fatalities in automotive or workplace accidents in terms of statistics, but if we decide that an algorithmic system should be designed to minimize accidents as a whole, we have to also judge any resulting harm in the context of the system it replaces.

The question is not how many humans were injured in an automated manufacturing facility or by a fleet of autonomous delivery vans, but rather how much more harm is likely to have been caused had the factory not had robots, or the delivery vans were being operated by overworked drivers, traveling through the night to reach their destination on time.

Leaders will be challenged by shareholders, customers, and regulators on what they optimize for. There will be lawsuits that require you to reveal the human decisions behind the design of your AI systems, what ethical and social concerns you took into account, and how well you monitored the results of those systems for traces of bias or discrimination. Document your decisions carefully and make sure you understand, or at the very least trust, the algorithmic processes at the heart of your business.

Simply arguing that your AI platform was a black box that no one understood is unlikely to be a successful legal defense in the twenty-first century. It will be about as convincing as *the algorithm made me do it.*

Focus on the forest, not just the trees

As an algorithmic leader, you can ask the right questions and make the right ethical choices, but still encounter another kind of algorithmic risk: abstraction.

Abstraction is a key part of how algorithmic systems work. You don't need to understand the detailed workings of every part of a computational system if you can trust the output of each layer. This trust allows programmers to work at higher levels of abstraction, without modifying the machine code at the bottom of the stack.

As organizations become more like algorithmic machines, there is a risk that their leaders will lose the ability to understand the end-to-end system. Isn't that the whole point of automation, you might ask? To reduce the cognitive load on leaders by taking away mechanical tasks and decisions so that they can focus on more pressing and complex issues?

Partly, yes. But it is never a good idea to only see trees and forget what a forest looks like. Even when you automate your processes, you need to retain the knowledge of how all the pieces fit together. Imagine a trading company that uses algorithms to handle every aspect of transactions, pricing, and market making. Its real risk is that over time, the only people who fully understand the complexity behind how the business operates are a handful of programmers, who might leave the company or end up working on increasingly fragmented and abstracted parts of the platform.

The next generation of leaders may be comfortable working alongside algorithmic and automated systems, but they also need to be mentored by the older generation that remembers the bigger picture: the hidden business logic and underlying complexity at the heart of any large organization.

The ability to question AI systems' design and data, to challenge their assumptions, and to bring deep knowledge and domain expertise to the discussion of their future are all powerful examples of the most important question that algorithmic leaders need to master: *Why?*

SUMMARY

1 As algorithms become more pervasive and capable of influencing human lives, algorithmic leaders need to be ready to ask, *Why?* Simply following the law is not an adequate moral compass in an

age when laws are unable to keep pace with disruptive change. If you want to avoid breaching the trust of your users and customers, you have to find a way to act in their best interest.

2 Algorithms are not impartial. They reflect our biases and viewpoints. The best way to avoid automating discrimination is to embrace diversity. Surround yourself with people who can help you understand the cultural context of your systems and data.

3 While we will continue to worry about our inability to fully understand how machines make decisions, algorithmic leaders will need to find workable compromises to ensure that they can get the benefit of machine learning, even when a system's recommendations are not entirely explicable.

4 Dumbing down AI platforms to the extent that we can actually understand them may undermine their effectiveness. It is often more important to know why a particular optimum or target was chosen than to be able to explain the reasoning behind an algorithmic decision.

5 As organizations become more like algorithmic machines, we risk losing the ability to comprehend their end-to-end systems. Don't lose sight of the complexities of your own business and the magic that lies in the detail of how things work.

QUESTION

If an AI causes a deadly mistake, who is ultimately culpable: the programmer who designed the algorithm, the data scientist who chose the training data, the safety engineer who failed to intervene, or you, the business leader who approved the optimization target?

WHEN IN DOUBT, ASK A HUMAN

*"Philosophically, intellectually—in every way—human
society is unprepared for the rise of artificial intelligence."*
HENRY KISSINGER

Humanize, don't standardize

Almost every company claims that its mission is to serve its customers. But what does "service" really mean when combined with algorithms and data? Does it mean standardizing and simplifying your product offering, or using your increased knowledge of your customers to offer a more complex, tailored service?

If you walk into Forward, located on a busy corner of Kearny and Sutter in San Francisco's Financial District, you could be forgiven for thinking that you had accidentally stumbled into an Apple Store. Or at least, a health clinic designed by Apple's retail team. And that is exactly the point. Asked to describe his health startup, founder Adrian Aoun explains that it should feel like a doctor's office that learns as it goes and applies lessons learned from data harvested from clients.

When you arrive for an appointment at Forward, you are scanned by a full-body scanner that checks multiple physical attributes and downloads the diagnostic data collected by your wearable devices about your physical activity levels and heart rate. Your personal data is then fed into an algorithm that is designed to identify and diagnose potential symptoms to help alert the health team to any latent issues that they should investigate.

By the time you actually enter the treatment room, the data from the scan and your wearable devices are ready to be viewed, manipulated, and interpreted by both you and the doctor on a large touch screen. The Forward connected health experience is a long way from the screaming children, old magazines, jars of stale jelly beans, and terrifying skeleton models that I remember from childhood visits to an overcrowded doctor's office. Forward offers a glimpse into the future, where data and algorithms combine with a human, personal way of delivering services.

As humans, we are complex and multifaceted. And yet as customers, clients, users, and patients, we are often treated by companies and platforms as one-dimensional transactions best described by a number. The old joke about banks (which still isn't that funny) was that they knew how many accounts they had, but not how many customers.

To understand why technology can have such a strong dehumanizing effect, you have to go back to the early days of mass production, when business processes, as well as manufacturing processes, started to be industrialized.

Standardization and simplification were major drivers of business design in the twentieth century. Henry Ford would sell you any color Model T you wanted, as long as it was black. Analogue leaders and companies were celebrated not for the diversity of customer experiences they created, but rather their ability to reduce costs and complexity, and create templates that could be replicated, franchised, and scaled globally. The service equation was actually a trade-off. Either serve a few customers with a lot of choices, or serve many by offering just a few choices.

When the Internet and digital commerce arrived, suddenly the calculus changed. The trade-off disappeared. You could provide a highly targeted, personalized experience—and at scale—without a dramatic increase in costs. Now leaders had a new problem: How do you understand the complexity of human behavior in all its variations and translate that into individualized experiences that matter?

In other words, how do you design your products and services with actual humans in mind?

Angela Ahrendts joined Apple as its senior vice president of Retail and Online Stores in 2014. She had pioneered the use of data and digital platforms at the luxury retailer Burberry but was still a newcomer to the world of selling consumer technology. When she joined, Apple Stores were already the number one store in the USA in terms of sales per square foot ($4,551), with their nearest rival being Tiffany & Co. ($3,132).

Even though Apple's sales per square foot continued to rise, exceeding $5,000 by 2018, Ahrendts's primary focus when she joined Apple was not to increase sales effectiveness but to redesign the company's retail operation to emphasize human connection and social interaction.

In late 2017, Ahrendts announced a big shift from the traditional Apple store to a new "town square" format. Rather than aisles, there would be "avenues" of products. Training rooms became "forums" for talks, while the largest stores would have "plazas" for concerts and events. Whereas you would previously have to wait in line at a Genius Bar for a technician to help you, there was now a tree-lined "genius grove" where you could wait and socialize. Some of Ahrendts's language, appropriated from urban planning, caused controversy. People reacted against the idea of "town squares," as it unintentionally highlighted just how much of public space was increasingly owned, and controlled, by private interests.

Yet Apple's move, while provocative, was consistent with a broader trend of a return to the humanization of retail experiences that involves the selective use of automation combined with the strategic use of human sales assistants, and the creation of immersive environments that respond to individual customers through their data.

Retailers in a digital age don't need stores, but digital retailers are building them anyway. Today's algorithmic store is not designed to simply sell things; it also serves as a platform to create relationships with customers.

Outdoor clothing brand Patagonia, for example, offers free yoga classes, hosts discussions on protecting the environment, and even puts on sewing workshops. Amazon's concept store in Seattle has no checkout lines and uses computer vision to identify the products you have taken from the shelves, billing your account automatically. It also has human agents around to provide advice and guidance. Nordstrom is testing a concept store in Los Angeles that doesn't sell merchandise at all, but instead offers services from stylists and tailors.

Nordstrom has long been a pioneer in the use of technology and data to humanize retail experiences. Early in 2011, it began rolling out mobile point of sale (POS) devices. The initial objective was to reduce customer wait time and lineups at checkouts. In an unexpected twist, it discovered that by reducing the amount of time that customers had to think about their purchases in this way, the number of abandoned transactions dropped and the average purchase price and number of items sold increased. That's the point of impulse buying, after all—if you can't act on an impulse, then you probably won't.

When it comes to selling complex or life-changing products like insurance or retirement solutions, being able to "ask a human" becomes important for a different reason: reassurance. You can use algorithms to create greater efficiency and simplicity in the delivery of your product, but the underlying feelings that people have about such products are not simple at all. We have human questions like, *What happens to my family if something happens to me?* Or *If someone breaks into my place and steals my stuff, what happens then?* All of these questions, many of them rooted in fear and anxiety, require either human support, or at the very least, a very sophisticated digital persona attuned to a client's personal needs and context.

While technology has generally supported the automation of business processes and the standardization of products and services, in the algorithmic age, leaders will be called upon to do the opposite: to create rich, immersive, personalized, and ultimately *human* experiences for their customers.

Look outside the window

It is not enough for us to understand complex human behavior. We have to help machines do the same.

Complex human behavior presents a challenge to algorithmic systems. When it comes to predicting human behavior, algorithmic systems are only as good as their ability to make sense of the world in front of them. Especially in new or ambiguous situations, learning algorithms can *overfit* a pattern to data, which is the machine equivalent of superstition.

Statistical models can become superstitious in the same way that we can. If on a few occasions a black cat crosses your path and bad things subsequently happen, you might start to assume that the two are linked. Machine learning algorithms can make the same mistake. Overfitting is caused by making a model more complex than necessary. If your model has too many variables and only a few observations from which the model can be learned, the algorithm can start to imagine patterns that are not real.

The complexity and nuances of human life can be hard for computers to gauge without human intervention to provide some context. That's why human perspective continues to be valuable, even in applications with a long history of automated decision making.

Ever since the Wright brothers first stood on the windswept dunes of Kitty Hawk, North Carolina, moments before their first flight in 1903, there has been a steady increase in the layers of automation between humans and the act of flying.

You can see this for yourself if you compare a picture of the cockpit of a modern Boeing 787 Dreamliner, with its simplified touch screens and controls, with that of an early 747, which had more than 1,000 instruments and switches. However, even in aviation, the relationship between humans and automated systems is a complicated one. There is a joke in the airline industry that the ideal flight crew is a pilot and a dog. The job of the pilot is to feed the dog, and the job of the dog is to bite the pilot if they try to touch any of the controls. Despite all the automation in a state-of-the-art aircraft, pilots will tell you that they like to occasionally look out the window to eyeball a challenging landing, check for the presence of other aircraft, or verify information from their instruments.

And yet, there is a good reason for why you might want a pilot to give their dog a biscuit and be able to take controls in certain circumstances. Computers lack common sense. We can train machine learning algorithms to spot patterns and detect signals, but to date we haven't been able to give them the ability to reason from context.

The famous algorithm trained by Andrew Ng and his team at Google, which was able to recognize a cat from watching YouTube videos, might have been able to discern the visual pattern of "cat" but it didn't know the context of a cat. For example, it didn't know that cats like to fight with dogs and hunt birds, or that they have a nonchalant relationship with their owners. Arguably, from that perspective, not even humans really understand cats. But we know a lot more than machines do.

Context is a complex issue. Some AI researchers believe that the only way we will teach algorithms to understand what they are doing is through Symbolic AI. Symbolic AI takes human-readable observations about the world and builds them into an expert system that allows a computer to make deductions and decisions. So, for example, if you wanted to help the YouTube cat detector become more informed about the subject of pet management, you might program in some of the hierarchy of how cats relate to birds and dogs. And, if you are brave, to their owners.

Symbolic AI had been, up until the 2012 ImageNet competition, the dominant approach for researchers attempting to create intelligent systems. John Haugeland gave the name GOFAI (Good Old-Fashioned Artificial Intelligence) to symbolic AI in his 1985 book, *Artificial Intelligence: The Very Idea.* Symbolic AI is very different from adaptive machine learning. It works on logic, rules, and structured input by human beings.

Future AI will most likely incorporate a mixture of both approaches. But regardless, humans will play a key role. Whether it is a domain specialist working with a machine learning programmer to adjust an algorithm that is making wrong predictions, or a symbolic logician devising a set of rules that approximate common sense, humans are essential when it comes to providing context to an AI.

A classic example is dealing with content. Content without context can easily be corrupted into becoming clickbait, fake news, or other forms of offensive material.

Between October and December 2017, YouTube took down 8 million videos. These videos, which contained terrorist content, hate speech, or other offensive material, represented a massive problem for Google, YouTube's parent company. Aside from ethical and political considerations, advertisers were growing worried about their brands potentially sharing the stage with inappropriate content. Although Google mainly uses algorithms and machine learning to remove content, the CEO of YouTube, Susan Wojcicki, committed in late 2017 to hiring a significant number of human beings to verify content, as well as full-time specialists with expertise in violent extremism, counterterrorism, and human rights.

Part of the reason for Google's strategy is that humans make good partners when it comes to training machine learning algorithms. In a blog post outlining YouTube's moderation strategy, Wojcicki explained that human reviewers remained essential to both removing content and training machine learning systems because human judgment was critical to making contextualized decisions on content.

Between June and December 2017, over 2 million videos were manually revised by YouTube's trust and safety teams. Those manual checks not only allowed them to assess whether the content in question actually violated their policies, they also—and more importantly—allowed them to train their algorithms to do a better job in the future.

Of course, there is no point in bringing in humans to eliminate bias and discriminatory content if your own culture lacks diversity. Wojcicki has long been an outspoken critic of the male-dominated culture in technology. Since she took over YouTube in 2014, she has increased the number of female employees there from 24 per cent to 30 per cent. Over that same period, the number of women working at Google has grown by just 1 per cent to 31 per cent.

Humans, however, are not only valuable in helping algorithms to spot offensive content; they can also help systems understand what other humans like to watch. One of the most coveted roles at Netflix is that of the originals creative analyst, commonly known as a Netflix tagger. The role typically involves watching up to twenty hours a week of Netflix and tagging episodes with relevant metadata, which is often quite a subjective exercise. While you can easily find basic facts about a film or TV show online, Netflix taggers spend time actually watching shows so that they can formulate more abstract concepts like the story line, genre, tone, and whether there are horror elements or a strong female lead. These human observations allow the Netflix algorithm to make more accurate and personalized recommendations for your viewing.

The music search engine Pandora did a very similar thing with their Music Genome Project. Over a decade, Pandora employed trained musicologists to listen to thousands of hours of diverse musical genres, classifying them according to a total of 450 musical attributes, which ultimately allowed the company to create automated, personalized listening experiences for their users that were unnervingly good.

As we delegate more decision-making power to algorithms to shape and govern the lives of humans, it will be equally important to ensure that we accurately reflect the complexity of human life in those systems, or at least provide the means for humans to identify and rectify mistakes.

Humans have a habit of thinking and acting in ways outside of expected norms, which can challenge algorithmic expectations. Anyone who has been hounded by their bank when they leave the country because its computer system thinks someone has stolen their credit card can attest to the frustrations of an algorithmic loop.

Soon algorithms will shape almost every aspect of our lives. They will determine our right to enter a country (US Customs now requires you to share your social media handles on request), buy train tickets (as happens with the social credit system in China), or shop at Amazon (Amazon can fire you as a customer if you start returning too many high-value items). Human judgment becomes very important if you want redress or challenge those decisions.

But as these systems grow more complex and harder to understand, the power of any human, as either a customer or employee, to contest an algorithmic decision becomes more difficult. And yet, that is exactly when your intervention becomes absolutely necessary. At that point, your livelihood may depend not on a machine, but on the ability of a person to look out the window and understand exactly what is going on.

Solve for everyone, not for the few

When I argue that humans are important, I don't just mean your customers. I also mean the people who could be your customers—namely, the people who were either too young, too costly, or too complicated to serve in the past. That's because the algorithmic age offers you the opportunity to think more broadly about who makes up the market for your services. Traditional companies, with rigid processes and structures, have less flexibility to serve low-margin or fragmented customer segments. Automation, thankfully, changes that calculation.

Whether it be health, finance, security, or transportation, for an algorithmic society to really work, it requires scale. By solving for everyone, across demographics, economics, and cultures, you gain the momentum and data to potentially win in your category. Amazon has become powerful as a retailer, not because it just sells to wealthy Americans, but because it provides a cost-effective, reliable delivery service to anyone in the US and many other countries too. Could the same logic apply to the delivery of financial advice and wealth management, a service typically utilized by the rich?

Ramya Joseph's father taught her from an early age that math was not about learning formulas and theorems but solving practical problems. He was an engineer who tried to instill in her a curiosity for numbers. At times, his passionate views made her life a little challenging. When she asked him to buy her an expensive calculator to do high school calculus, he laughed at her and said, "I'm not buying you that calculator. You don't need a calculator to do integrals." So she learned to do them without one.

When I visited Pefin, the company that Joseph founded in New York City, I was bemused to see a giant table at the front entrance, stacked high with dog-eared books. For a technology startup, it was like a slightly ironic memorial to the analogue age. Among the varied titles were a biography of Elon Musk and several books by Michael Lewis.

"Ah, I see you found our lending library," she said with a smile, as she greeted me. "These are not for me. I read on my Kindle."

After finishing school, Joseph earned two master's degrees from Columbia University, one in artificial intelligence and the other in financial engineering. She co-filed her first patent at the age of twenty-three in the area of software architecture.

With a background in computer science and finance, Joseph was a natural fit for a newly tech-focused Wall Street and soon found herself in a relatively new area called algorithmic trading. At about that time, in the early 1990s, electronic trading started to transform the finance industry. Algorithmic trading went from 15 per cent of trading volume to 20 per cent, and then to over 90 per cent. Soon, she found herself managing multibillion-dollar portfolios on Wall Street, first at Morgan Stanley, and later as vice president of Proprietary Trading at Goldman Sachs. Then the financial crisis of 2008 hit. Joseph didn't lose her job, but her father did.

Joseph's father, who was sixty, was suddenly faced with the prospect of unplanned early retirement. After years of helping millionaires manage their money, Joseph realized that her father, like many other middle-class people impacted by the financial crisis, also needed expert help.

Both her parents were highly intelligent, educated people. Her father had a double master's degree, and her mom had a PhD. However, when it comes to financial decisions, the sheer volume of factors that can affect your financial outcome is mind-boggling. Even for brilliant people. So Joseph put together a massive Excel spreadsheet for them. It took her two weeks. The spreadsheet looked at everything from Medicare to social security, her father's benefits to her mom's grocery shopping. Finally, she sat down with her father and explained all the options she had modeled for him. His relief was palpable. Suddenly, he could see a way past the crisis to a solution.

The reason Joseph's father still struggled to make financial decisions was that financial institutions are often set up to sell products rather than solve problems. They were ready to sell him an annuity or a variable life insurance policy, but they couldn't answer the question of whether he could retire—at least, not without purchasing something from them. Like many families, their needs fell into the gap between simple, off-the-shelf solutions and the kinds of bespoke strategies that only the wealthy could obtain with help from teams of professional advisers.

That got Joseph thinking. How might you scale financial advice and offer it in a way that was not only fiduciary, with a no-strings-attached policy, but also affordable? It took her six months to frame the problem and investigate the technology that she would need before she felt confident enough to quit her job and launch her business. And that was the beginning of Pefin, an AI financial adviser.

Pefin is a feed-forward neural network. It takes a client's behavior and transactions as an input, processes that information through a series of interconnected nodes that understand financial rules and relationships, and produces an output or a financial plan. Any time the client's data changes, such as when they have a child or buy a house, the network automatically updates its projections and plans. The system learns from a client's actual behavior, rather than their ideas or plans, and tailors its recommendations accordingly.

Joseph's platform is like having a highly paid adviser on retainer, except that the insights are being delivered by an algorithm, at scale, to millions of people in a highly personalized way.

See the world as a designer

In a self-driving car, the most dangerous moment is not when the car starts driving itself, but rather in those critical moments when the control needs to be handed back to a human being. In that instant, when the center of control shifts, if the driver is unprepared, reacts in an unpredictable way, or lacks experience due to overreliance on automation, the results can be fatal.

The successful handoff between automated systems and manual control is reliant not on processing power or accurate sensors but on design. Seeing the world through the eyes of a designer allows algorithmic leaders to anticipate not only how people might act in a particular situation, but also to understand the true human needs that should be the focus of any platform.

For AI to be useful, it has to solve problems in a practical way. Algorithms can't figure out the right problems to solve without input from people adept at identifying and correctly framing human needs. That's why companies that build AI systems for consumer use are starting to rely on a new discipline called human-centered machine learning. This form of design-thinking blends the hard work of finding out what people need (ethnography, contextual inquiries, interviews, observation, surveys, reading customer support tickets, logs analysis) with an iterative approach to software engineering and interface design.

The idea is that by thinking like a designer, you can make systems more useful and relevant. Designers focus on the people who will use their products, and their needs and behavior. To do this, they apply human factors, ergonomics, and contextual knowledge to the design of interfaces, interaction models, and the actual algorithms. As a blog post written by Google's design team explains, human-centered design is a lens for how machine learning can stay grounded in human needs while solving them in unique ways only possible through machine learning.

Some of the questions that Google engineers ask when designing an algorithmic system are:

- How might a theoretical human "expert" perform the task today?
- If your human expert were to perform this task, how would you respond to them so they improved for the next time?
- If a human were to perform this task, what assumptions would the user want them to make?

Thinking like a designer is more complex than trying to create an aesthetically pleasing user interface. While software engineering has established processes for writing code, we are still in the early stages of figuring out the workflow for building AI platforms and applications. Andrew Ng provides a good example of this in his machine learning online course, when he describes the problem of designing an AI chatbot.

If you were a product manager at a technology company, how would you explain to a software engineer how a new chatbot should work? If you were to approach the problem in the same way you would approach a mobile application or a Web page, you might draw a wireframe to explain the functionality that you need. However, in the case of an AI chatbot, this would just be a series of chat balloons. Your wireframe would not communicate either the complexity of the interactions or how an AI should respond in different situations.

When he faced this issue at Baidu, Ng asked his product managers and engineers to sit down together and write out fifty conversations that a chatbot might have with a user. This process of imagining the human experience created a conversation between the product manager and the engineer around the extent of the features required to enable the manager to identify what users would love and the engineer to specify what was feasible.

To further deepen the interactions between his product team and engineers, Ng would also encourage product managers to come up with datasets of things that really mattered to them. Using data is an effective way for product people to communicate with technical people. For example, in speech recognition, a product manager might need to come up with 10,000 audio recordings that include audio features like noisy car environments, background noise in cafés, accented speech, or any other attributes that they think might interfere with the operation of their service. As with the example conversations for a new chatbot design, working with sample data bridges the gap between an abstract human need and concrete decisions that impact the design and engineering of a product.

Thinking like a designer also means anticipating and responding to user behavior as it changes over time. One of the unique challenges with designing adaptive systems that learn and evolve is having to take into account a user's mental model. When users interact with an AI system, they are also influencing the kinds of outputs they will see in the future. Those adjustments, in turn, impact how other users interact with the system, and so on, creating a feedback loop. Sometimes these loops are called *conspiracy theories*, because users end up with an incorrect mental model of a system and then try to manipulate the outputs according to the rules they have dreamed up. They are not trying to hack your system, they are just operating on a false premise of how it works because you have not designed the interactions clearly enough.

Avoiding conspiracy theories is an important aspect of successful algorithmic design. If you open Netflix, you may notice that your recommendations come with an explanation. The interface explains that they are recommending that you watch more British period dramas because you previously watched *The Crown*. This helps avoid you thinking that Netflix somehow thinks that you might like these shows because you have a common English surname, that you were researching holidays in the Cotswolds, or you had previously bought tickets to a Renaissance Faire.

A vital part of any algorithmic system is providing users with clear mental models that encourage them to behave in a way that is mutually beneficial to both them and the platform. For future designers, it also illustrates the importance of thinking beyond aesthetics and preparing yourself to be able to shape the interaction models and experiences of how humans use AI products.

Augment relationships, don't replace them

Professor Geoffrey Hinton, whose team won the 2012 ImageNet competition (see chapter 2), caused quite a stir in the health community when he observed that radiologists were "the coyote already over the edge of the cliff who hasn't yet looked down." In Hinton's view, we should stop training radiologists, as image recognition algorithms were soon going to be demonstrably better at the job than humans. The problem with Hinton's prediction is that it ignores what radiologists actually do. In fact, when algorithms automate the repetitive and straightforward tasks played by healthcare professionals, rather than replacing them, it frees up the professionals to spend more time on truly valuable activities.

Dr. Hugh Harvey is a next-generation medical professional, with one foot in the world of frontline healthcare and the other in that of machine learning and algorithms. He has worked both as a radiologist and as the head of regulatory affairs at Babylon Health. He is currently the clinical director at a new AI startup called Kheiron Medical, which is using deep learning to help doctors identify breast cancer earlier. Harvey believes that AI will not replace radiologists but will instead augment their capabilities and allow them to focus on the human-level interactions that matter.

When I asked him what the job of a twenty-first-century radiologist should be, Harvey replied, "I think that radiologists are going to go from being these crude 'lumpologists,' or people who are just looking at lumps and measuring them, to becoming data wranglers. They will be looking at the outputs from various algorithms all at once, combining these and making an inference and a diagnostic judgment based on the data."

In Harvey's opinion, AI is going to change radiology, rather than replace radiologists. Algorithmic systems would allow radiologists to monitor and assess machine outputs, rather than manually going through every possible finding. Harvey explained that he had wasted much of his professional life measuring lymph nodes on multiple CT scans or counting vertebrae to report the level of a metastasis. He would rather use his time to check that a system has measured the correct lymph nodes and identified all the vertebrae required, and then sign off on the findings.

By augmenting the role of radiologists through machine learning, Harvey believes they will become more like data specialists whose primary function is communicating and collaborating with both clinicians and patients. Communicating data well requires balancing an understanding of sophisticated tools with the ability to translate complex findings in a way that focuses on the most important issues and insights.

A similar transformation may occur in sales and account management–type jobs. Algorithms have the potential to automate almost every aspect of sales, from identifying prospects to creating proposals, setting rates, handling contracts, and sending out reminders for renewals. That doesn't mean, however, that the human side of selling can be completely replaced. If anything, just like in radiology, automation creates an opportunity to invest more in relationships and communication.

Even in industries like finance or commodities where automated trading has become commonplace, algorithms haven't completely replaced the role of humans. You might be able to use algorithms to measure the risk and to set prices, but the relationship with a counterparty, distributor, or supplier doesn't go away.

Selling is a uniquely human capability and difficult to fully automate. That's because we not only sell products, we also sell ourselves. Part of brokering a complex relationship between two organizations is not just aligning technical details, it is also communicating a shared vision and convincing others to get on board with you. Machines may be able identify the optimal structure of a deal, but if you want your investors, partners, and customers to really believe in it, you will need something more.

You will need to ask a human.

SUMMARY

1 While technology allows companies to standardize and simplify their offerings, the most successful organizations in the algorithmic age will embrace the complexity of human behavior and translate it into individualized, immersive experiences.

2 Algorithmic systems lack common sense, so avoiding dangerous errors, bias, or unacceptable choices typically requires input based on human judgment. In the future, the ability to reach a human who is empowered to override an algorithmic decision may be vital to our safety or livelihood.

3 AI should not be just a product for a privileged few, but a platform to provide services for the many. The story of Ramya Joseph and her company, Pefin, illustrates how AI can deliver tailored financial advice to everyone. Equity is not the only issue. Given the importance of scale to data-driven systems, algorithmic leaders need to rethink their assumptions about the customer segments that they can profitably serve.

4 To properly address human needs, we need to develop the discipline of human-centered design for machine learning. For AI to be useful, it has to solve problems for people in a practical and empathetic way.

5 It might be able to automate work, but AI can't override the importance of human relationships. By freeing us up from repetitive tasks, AI can give us the choice to focus on the human interactions that really matter.

QUESTION

If you can automate most of your product or service delivery, how can you best use human beings to enhance the overall customer experience?

SOLVE FOR PURPOSE, NOT JUST PROFIT

*"Work gives you meaning and purpose,
and life is empty without it."*
STEPHEN HAWKING

Connect people to their work

We work for many reasons. Some of the more common ones are the need to pay our bills and put food on the table, or a desire to fund certain lifestyle choices. But if you take a step back and look at human civilization as a whole, you'll realize that there are infinite ways that our needs and desires can be taken care of without us working, in some cases, an eighty-hour week.

Many of my colleagues and friends are advocates of paying everyone a universal basic income (UBI). A UBI would mean a radical change to the design of our economy. It might address rising issues of inequality and algorithmic unemployment. Or it might not. Personally, I'm not entirely convinced of its potential. As Luke Martinelli, a researcher at the University of Bath's Institute for Policy Research, has written, "an affordable UBI is inadequate, and an adequate UBI is unaffordable." In either case, a UBI is unlikely to do much to alleviate one of the deeper implications of widespread automation: the loss of human purpose.

Even if we could radically design the economy and leverage technology to take care of all of our material needs, it is possible that people would still feel alienated, depressed, bored, or disengaged when their usual work is taken away from them. While we might like to believe that we work to live, rather than live to work, the more we understand about our biochemical engineering and the reward systems of our brain, the more apparent it is that we have to work in order for our lives to have meaning and purpose.

Work is where we form a sense of identity. It is how we leverage the skills and experience we have gained over the years, and where we can see the results of our efforts. You don't have to be a champion skier, the CEO of a global corporation, or a rock star for your labors to have personal significance. You just have to connect with your work in a way that provides meaning and a sense of overall purpose.

Those who argue for a UBI point out that with the mass automation of work, and our robot overlords addressing our material needs, humans will finally be free to find meaning and purpose in other activities. In a way, something similar happened almost 3,000 years ago. Would we have had the explosion of art and culture in the classical world without the gains in productivity and efficiency that those societies had also achieved?

Thales of Miletus, who was one of the Seven Sages of Greece and is sometimes called the father of Western philosophy, observed that he was able to devote time to thinking about the world because his society had perfected the practical arts: cultivating crops, herding animals, building high-walled cities, navigating the seas, and defending themselves with well-trained armies. The time freed up by all this efficiency made it possible for him to focus on philosophy instead of being bothered with the practical arts. Of course, presumably those busy in the fields, tending the animals, laying stones, sailing ships, and killing enemies had a different take on life. The classical world had automation too. It took the form of slaves.

I don't buy the idea of a world of automated abundance arriving anytime soon. In my view, the real risk of living in an algorithmic society is not that we will have too much time on our hands and nothing to do, but rather that the nature of work will suddenly atomize to the extent that we lose perspective on why we are doing it. The alienation of the worker, a concept that provided popular support for Karl Marx's *Communist Manifesto* and the revolution that followed it, was a direct result of the fragmented nature of work following the Industrial Revolution.

Suddenly, skilled artisans, who had trained for years in perfecting the manufacture of an object or a piece of clothing, were replaced by a production line made up of thousands of relatively unskilled workers, managed like cogs in a machine. They were given tiny, specialized tasks, like assembling a single component over and over again, without any sense of why it even mattered.

Although many employees in organizations today are not factory workers but knowledge workers, there is still the risk of alienation. The desire to reconnect people to the purpose of their work was one of the primary drivers behind Dutch bank ING's decision in 2015 to start a company-wide, agile transformation that empowered its employees to deliver more customer-relevant products, more quickly and flexibly. Inspired by algorithmic companies like Google, Netflix, and Spotify, ING took the radical step of creating 350 nine-person squads, each focused on a specific customer objective. These squads were then affiliated with thirteen tribes (squads with interconnected missions) to ensure that the company kept pushing toward bigger goals.

To learn more about the results of their transformation, I spoke with Peter Jacobs, CIO of ING Bank, and one of the original architects of its transformation program. He explained that people in large companies can lose their sense of purpose if complex projects are broken down into smaller components and the process is essentially turned into virtual assembly lines. That prevents employees from gaining a sense of accountability or ownership over the ultimate objective.

"Imagine that you are a brilliant, twenty-five-year-old marketer or engineer. The organization will tell you, 'You are so special. We would like you to work on the most relevant project that we have.' And you go home and your partner asks you, 'Hey, when will you have an impact?' You say, 'Oh, I forgot to ask.' Then you go back the next day and your colleague tells you, 'Well, the first time your customers will enjoy what you're doing is in four years from now.' You have basically killed purpose. You've killed it immediately by the way that you organize yourself."

For Jacobs, the key to reigniting a sense of purpose was to bring back the idea of craftsmanship. People not only need to understand the rationale for their work, they also have to be able to see it through from start to finish. In Jacobs's view, sometimes it is better to give people a broader role in a smaller project, because that can help them feel as if they own the results.

"Part of recognizing that people are special," Jacobs continued, "is that you don't give them impositions; you give them objectives. You don't tell them that they need to build a bridge; you say to them, let's think together about how to cross the river."

It is not only about your team members needing a rationale for their work; it is equally about you needing to find the right rationale for your company's transformation. Leading change in an organization is never easy. It can be political, unpredictable, and terrifying for those involved. If you want people to come along with you for the journey, it helps if you can give them a reason for why they need to change. Achieving higher profits, lower costs, more market share, or even corporate survival are not as motivating as you might think—none of those are why people work in the first place.

The primary driver of your digital transformation should be purpose rather than profits, but that doesn't mean that you need to become a charity or connect your company mission to something that is going to save the world. To be completely honest, I find the idea of every company having a *massively transformative purpose* kind of ridiculous.

Not every company needs to end world hunger, save the environment, or bring unbridled joy into the universe. Sometimes, it is okay to just make high-quality toilet paper, reliable rubber sealants, or a decent cup of coffee.

Connecting people to their work doesn't mean you need to window-dress the nature of your work. It is fine to do something mundane and profitable. If you can use technology to do it efficiently while providing a humane and respectful environment for people to work, a place where their contributions are recognized and valued, then you will have done more than enough for the world.

And more importantly, for your people.

Beware the algorithmic inequality trap

"In the future, you will be either working for the algorithm or if you are lucky, on the algorithm," explained Sean Gourley grimly, as we sat drinking a cup of green tea in Tokyo.

Gourley and I were both speaking at an event, and I had just finished interviewing him for my podcast. Gourley has led a fascinating life. Originally from New Zealand, he gained a PhD in physics from Oxford University. As part of his academic research on complex systems, he studied the "mathematics of war" and served as a political adviser to the Pentagon and the UN on predicting conflict. His speciality was identifying networks of insurgents. He also founded two AI companies, one that focused on data visualization and the other on machine intelligence.

Although Gourley was enthusiastic about the prospect of humans and machines working together effectively, he was also cautious about a future in which a class-based divide could open up between the masses who effectively had some kind of algorithm as their boss (think of Uber drivers), a privileged professional class who had the skills and capabilities to design and train algorithmic systems, and a tiny, almost aristocratic class of the ultra-wealthy, who actually owned the algorithmic platforms.

You can already see glimpses of a low-paid, algorithmic workforce emerging around the world. In Latin America, one of the fastest-growing startups is Rappi, a mix of Uber Eats, Instacart, and TaskRabbit. Customers in cities like Bogotá and Mexico City pay about $1 an order or a flat $7 a month, and in return can access a vast on-demand network of couriers who deliver food, groceries, and just about anything else you want. Amazon has its own informal network of delivery people, called Amazon Flex, who in the near future will do everything that drones can't do effectively, whether it be hand parcels to you in the street or place them in your car trunk, or even open the door to your house and store your groceries in your fridge. Amazon estimates that in the next few years, Amazon Flex will employ over 1 million people worldwide.

What happens when more and more people are employed as part of a transient workforce governed by algorithms? These courier nomads may have the latest holographic phones, bone-conduction headphones, and low-latency, augmented reality eyewear, but make no mistake, they will be the physical manifestation of a new algorithmic underclass. Yes, it is good news that there will still be work for humans to do. But if the conditions in and protections from that work are not sufficient for a dignified life in the twenty-first century, there will be devastating social and political consequences for everyone involved.

In his 1930 lecture *Economic Possibilities for Our Grandchildren*, John Maynard Keynes predicted that by around 2030, the production problem would be solved and there would be enough of everything for everyone. The catch, however, is that machines would cause "technological unemployment." The scenario that Keynes didn't fully anticipate was a case of high technological employment, with an accompanying degree of high inequality.

Even within organizations, you will find growing inequality and a widening gap between top executives and an outer fringe of transient workers. In the future, in data-driven companies like Amazon or Walmart, you may end up with a small cohort of very highly paid employees who are supported by sophisticated automation and a large group of low-paid freelancers.

Nevertheless, it is dangerous to try to fix a problem that is yet to fully manifest. Already, governments and regulators supported by populist platforms are focused on attacking global digital giants. They seek to prevent them from avoiding tax liabilities, and are working to regulate the labor conditions of their freelance workforce, apply restrictions on their collection of data, and even tax their robots. Some of these ideas have merit. Others are premature, or worse, just political theater.

The longer-term solution to algorithmic inequality will not lie in just taxation and regulation, but rather in our ability to provide an adequate education system for the twenty-first century. *We will reap what we teach.* It may take a while to show, but there will be a noticeable gap between those countries that invest in the future capabilities of their workforce and those that try to focus only on short-term, political gains. This gap might be best measured by a ratio of algorithmic inequality, or the ratio of how many citizens are working for, rather than working on, the algorithms that power a country's platforms and services.

Use algorithmic management thoughtfully

Algorithms might allow you to manage more people at scale, but that doesn't mean they will make you a better manager. In the name of efficiency, progress, and scalability (and all the other gods of transformation), you might be encouraged to let algorithms manage more and more of your interactions with your teams.

A word of advice: *don't.*

Sure, you can use an algorithm to set your work rosters so that the number of hours is just below the legal threshold for full-time employment, automatically send emails to people when they are more than five minutes late to work, nudge people to work during the time they normally spend with their families by offering incentives, use sensors to monitor your warehouse workers and notify them when they are taking longer than the average time to stack a shelf, or constantly adjust the color temperature of your office lighting so that your employee's circadian system thinks that late afternoon is still morning. All those things are already possible, and in some companies, even pending. But in the end, they will backfire on you.

We have been here before. About a hundred years ago, the world experienced the Scientific Management revolution, or more popularly, Taylorism. US industrial engineer Frederick Winslow Taylor had a lot of ideas about how companies might integrate machine and worker for maximum efficiency, and he wrote them all down in his 1911 book, *The Principles of Scientific Management.*

Many principles of Taylorism are being revived today with a digital or AI-based twist. Consider this list of ideas: empirical data collection; process analysis; efficiency; elimination of waste; standardization of best practices; disdain for tradition; mass production and scale; and knowledge transfer between workers and from workers into tools, processes, and documentation. That might sound like a twenty-first-century digital transformation plan, but they are all ideas that Taylor had all those decades ago, and they led to unfortunate ends, including worker alienation, industrial action, and falling productivity.

Unfortunately, we are likely to see the return of many of these ideas in the algorithmic age. Amazon, for example, has received two patents for a wristband designed to guide warehouse workers' movements with the use of vibrations to nudge them into being more efficient. IBM has also applied for a patent for a system that monitors its workforce with sensors that can track pupil dilation and facial expressions and then use data on an employee's sleep quality and meeting schedule to deploy drones to deliver a jolt of caffeinated liquid so its employees' workday is undisturbed by a coffee break.

Just like Taylorism, overreliance on algorithmic management may end up creating unease in the workplace and broader social unrest. Industrial action may grow, in which case regulators will have to consider intervention. In coming years, the leaders in your organization will be forced to confront such issues as well. There will almost certainly be a debate about whether it is better to reduce the agency of human beings by directing their actions entirely by AI, versus having more distributed, autonomous teams.

The sad reality, from a purely economic standpoint, is that both approaches may be right, depending on the industry and the capabilities of the workforce. As to what the right balance should be, that is exactly the kind of subtle dilemma that algorithmic leaders like you will be equipped to handle. Just use the algorithms thoughtfully. One day, they may be used on you too.

Build platforms that you would use yourself

In the future, we won't work for companies. We'll work for platforms. The difference is not just semantic, and it will not apply only to junior-level jobs. As people start to demand more flexibility in their working arrangements and companies need to be more flexible in their approach to attracting the right talent to solve problems, at almost every level of the organization, we will need to start behaving more like freelancers rather than full-time employees.

Many companies are already becoming platforms for talent. A company like Uber doesn't hire people, it provides a platform for people to create value as drivers. Even AT&T, with its skills training platform, is preparing for a world in which there isn't a career ladder but a *career lattice*, where valued employees can leverage their skills in nonlinear ways, across a range of jobs and challenges over the course of their tenure. At Satalia, Daniel Hulme and his team are attempting to use machine learning to assign problems and decisions to people with the right capabilities to solve and make them.

We will see more algorithmic matching of talent, not just for Uber drivers and delivery people but for professionals and experts as well. Publicis, a multinational marketing company, has already started using algorithms to organize and assign its 80,000 employees, including account managers, coders, graphic designers, and copywriters. Whenever there is a new project or client pitch, the algorithm recommends the right combination of talent for the best possible result.

Of course, the design of talent platforms is also open to manipulation and abuse. Some retailers have attracted criticism for erratic and unfair work schedules created by automated software systems. Automated work scheduling can be a powerful tool to help companies manage their costs, whether that means sending workers home when sales are slowing, or rapidly staffing up when the weather changes or there is a seasonal promotion. It can also be structured to help an organization avoid certain obligations. In August 2013, for example, less than two weeks after the teen-fashion chain Forever 21 began using Kronos, a workforce optimization platform, hundreds of full-time workers were notified that they'd be switched to part-time and that their health benefits would be terminated.

The fairest way to design a talent platform that encompasses the entire hierarchy of your company, from your junior positions all the way up to your top leaders is to imagine that everyone, from top to bottom, has to be governed by the same principles. The Veil of Ignorance was a thought experiment proposed in 1971 by US philosopher John Rawls. He proposed a theory that the best way for people to make political or social decisions with far-reaching impact is for them to imagine how they would feel about those decisions if they woke up the next morning and found that they were one of the people who were directly affected and had had no input into the decision. Algorithmic leaders should take the same approach when building systems that manage their own teams and employees.

AI and algorithms offer a wealth of opportunities to design more flexible, fulfilling ways to work. Just be sure that you would be prepared to use the same talent platform you are expecting other people to use.

Transform work by transforming yourself

The journey to becoming an algorithmic leader is fundamentally one of personal accountability.

Transformation cannot be bought. It is easy to go through the motions of digital transformation: you can hire a team of expensive consultants to deliver a fancy strategy presentation for your board, offer free coding lessons for your employees, upgrade to the latest enterprise technology stack, and even buy a few promising AI startups and integrate them into your business. But in the end, the likelihood of your organization becoming a successful, twenty-first-century organization depends on the culture you create through your actions and the way you empower the people around you.

To transform work, you have to change the way you work. And to do that, you have to find a personal connection to your own purpose for doing so. If your company's motivation for radical reinvention is simply to increase profit or gain market share, while you might publicly support the program, secretly you, and those around you, will probably end up doing exactly the opposite. Before you can transform your organization, you have to look within yourself to find the reason for how and why things should change.

What excites me most about the idea of an algorithmic leader is that it offers people a *tabula rasa*, a blank canvas to reimagine what they do. Whether you are just starting your career or are an industry veteran, whether you are an executive in a big company or work alone as a freelancer, we are all at a turning point, and it is essential that we reevaluate and reimagine our purpose and potential.

In the next few years, jobs and careers that were unimaginable a decade ago will be the norm. Refik Anadol, a friend of mine, is now one of the world's most accomplished data sculptors—a job that didn't exist until very recently. Originally from Turkey, Anadol studied a wide range of media and visual design disciplines, but it was his early exposure to an old VHS tape of *Blade Runner* that led him to wonder whether algorithms and data could transform the way we create art.

In recent years, Anadol has collaborated with Frank Gehry and the Los Angeles Philharmonic to display projection-map designs on the inside of the Hollywood Bowl, its home, that respond in real time to the musical performance and the actions of the conductor. Later, as an artist-in-residence at Google, he worked with their machine learning teams to transform a Turkish archive of over 1.7 million documents from the Ottoman era into an AI installation called *Archive Dreaming*. The 6-meter (18-foot) wide circular installation uses machine learning algorithms to search, organize, and display pieces from the collection. You can use the interface to browse the items in the library, but when it is idle, the installation "dreams" of unexpected correlations among its own documents.

"I find it extremely inspiring," Anadol explained when we spoke, "because if you think about the near future of the architecture, facades and spaces, the skin of a building may gain a kind of a knowledge from machine intelligence. Buildings will remember the memories of an institution, and hallucinate a future that does not yet exist."

To be an algorithmic leader means more than simply becoming the digital version of yourself. It means opening yourself to entirely new ideas that could never have become a reality before an age of artificial intelligence.

A short time ago, I had the opportunity to present some of the ideas in this book to the top 200 global leaders at Deutsche Telekom, the largest telecommunications provider in Europe, at their T3 management summit held in the picturesque town of Alpbach, high in the Austrian Alps. When I finished, Tim Höttges, the CEO of the company, approached me in the corridor and shared an interesting observation.

"I know a lot of the algorithmic leaders you mentioned," he said with a smile. "You know, they weren't always that way. Many of them started out as pretty analogue. The difference is, they made a conscious decision to change, to surround themselves with the right people, and to do things differently."

Algorithms are just a tool. There are no robot overlords coming for your job, unless you choose to create some. For now at least, humans remain in the driver's seat, making decisions about what happens next. Some of those decisions you will make; others will be made for you. Some may impact you and your career in the very near future; others may take years to manifest. While you can't control all of those factors, what you can do is *start today* by changing the way you approach problems and make decisions.

You are not alone. You are part of a network of other leaders on a quest for growth and reinvention. The complexity of the algorithmic age defies simple solutions or solitary heroes. Only when we work together, empowered by new ways of thinking, with smart machines to guide us, and a renewed sense of our value, can we truly transform our organizations, our industries, and the world itself.

SUMMARY

1 Work is more than just meeting our material needs; it is connected to our sense of identity and purpose. As we use more algorithms in the workplace, there is a risk that people will lose their connection to the value and rationale behind their labor.

2 In the future, we will be either working for or on the algorithm. Avoiding the algorithmic inequality trap will require more than just new forms of taxation or regulation; it will also need a sustained investment in training and education by both companies and countries.

3 Algorithmic management has the potential to revive the evils of Taylorism and, unless handled carefully, global social unrest and industrial action.

4 We will all be working for talent platforms in the future, whether as freelancers or as flexible employees in a global organization. Leaders have an obligation to design platforms that they themselves would be comfortable using.

5 The journey to transformation begins and ends with you. Most of us started out as analogue leaders. It will take a conscious application of persistence, patience, and will to fulfill what the future wants from us: *to become algorithmic leaders.*

QUESTION

If you no longer needed to work to live, what would you do for free?

EPILOGUE

The greatest danger in writing books about the future is not being wrong, but taking too long to be right. To avoid that fate, I've focused on principles rather than predictions. There is nothing inevitable about the future. Whether we end up in a world run by empowered human leaders or algorithmic overlords largely depends on you and what you do next.

Throughout this book, I've asked you to reflect on how algorithmic leaders think and act differently to their analogue predecessors.

In my view, algorithmic leaders:

- Focus on their future customers, not their existing ones
- Design their operating model for multipliers, not margins
- Analyze problems from first principles, not by analogy
- Seek to be less wrong with time, rather than always being right
- Humanize and complexify, rather than standardize and simplify
- Are guided by user empowerment, rather than mere regulatory compliance
- Ask whether they have the right approach, rather than whether they are getting results
- Manage by principles, rather than processes
- Believe that they should automate and elevate, rather than automate and decimate
- Transform for purpose, not just profit

These points should not be seen as a definitive checklist on how to be a successful leader; they're a starting point for your own journey. In the same way that business complexity resists complete automation, human leadership defies simple definition. Although the algorithmic world continually makes new demands on how we approach problems, decisions, and opportunities, we all need to find our own path to transformation.

I hope the stories in this book give you a sense of how a small but growing group of leaders are transforming themselves and the people around them. They are not the leaders we grew up with, or even the ones we may have hoped for, but they are the ones we need, the ones who will lead us in an age of smart machines.

ACKNOWLEDGMENTS

A book about the future is only as good as the people in the present who make it possible. I'm grateful to Jesse Finkelstein and her wonderful team at Page Two who helped bring my idea to life, in particular my patient and insightful editor, Amanda Lewis, and my copy editor, Lesley Cameron. A very special thanks to my agent and mentor, Karen Harris, and all her amazing people at CMI Speaker Management who have been on this journey of transformation and big ideas with me since the very beginning. Most of all, I'd like to thank my beautiful wife, Burcu, who not only listened to my crazy ramblings but also helped me forge them into fully formed thoughts. She is, and always will be, my muse.

REFERENCES
AND FURTHER READING

Introduction | Welcome to the algorithmic age

Andreessen, Marc. "This Is Probably a Good Time to Say that I Don't Believe Robots Will Eat All the Jobs." Marc Andreessen Blog. June 13, 2014. blog.pmarca.com/2014/06/13/this-is-probably-a-good-time-to-say-that-i-dont-believe-robots-will-eat-all-the-jobs

Arthur, W. Brian. "Where Is Technology Taking the Economy?" *McKinsey Quarterly*. McKinsey & Company. October 2017. mckinsey.com/business-functions/mckinsey-analytics/our-insights/where-is-technology-taking-the-economy

Bessen, James E. "Automation and Jobs: When Technology Boosts Employment." Boston University School of Law, Law and Economics Research Paper No. 17-09. March 23, 2018. ssrn.com/abstract=2935003

———. "The Automation Paradox." *Atlantic*. January 19, 2016. theatlantic.com/business/archive/2016/01/automation-paradox/424437

———. "How Computer Automation Affects Occupations: Technology, Jobs, and Skills." Boston University School of Law, Law and Economics Research Paper No. 15-49. October 3, 2016. ssrn.com/abstract=2690435

Byrnes, Nanette. "As Goldman Embraces Automation, Even the Masters of the Universe Are Threatened." *MIT Technology Review*. February 7, 2017. technologyreview.com/s/603431/as-goldman-embraces-automation-even-the-masters-of-the-universe-are-threatened

Chui, Michael, James Manyika, and Mehdi Miremadi. "What AI Can and Can't Do (Yet) for Your Business." *McKinsey Quarterly*. McKinsey & Company. January 2018. mckinsey.com/business-functions/mckinsey-analytics/our-insights/what-ai-can-and-cant-do-yet-for-your-business

Detrixhe, John. "Lesson from the Cupcake ATM: Better to Be a Baker Than a Seller." Quartz. July 4, 2017. qz.com/1014632/lesson-from-the-cupcake-atm-better-to-be-a-baker-than-a-seller

Gershgorn, Dave. "The Data That Transformed AI Research—and Possibly the World." Quartz. July 26, 2017. qz.com/1034972/the-data-that-changed-the-direction-of-ai-research-and-possibly-the-world

———. "DeepMind Has a Bigger Plan for Its Newest Go-Playing AI." Quartz. October 18, 2017. qz.com/1105509/deepminds-new-alphago-zero-artificial-intelligence-is-ready-for-more-than-board-games

Lee, Kai-Fu. "Tech Companies Should Stop Pretending AI Won't Destroy Jobs." *MIT Technology Review*. February 21, 2018. technologyreview.com/s/610298/tech-companies-should-stop-pretending-ai-wont-destroy-jobs

Lynch, Clifford. "Stewardship in the Age of Algorithms." *First Monday* 22 (12). December 4, 2017. http://firstmonday.org/ojs/index.php/fm/article/view/8097/6583

Ray, Shaan. "The Emergence of Artificial Intelligence." Towards Data Science. February 5, 2018. towardsdatascience.com/the-emergence-of-artificial-intelligence-3cde7378768e

Robb, John. "How Algorithms and Authoritarianism Created a Corporate Nightmare at United." Newco Shift. April 17, 2017. shift.newco.co/2017/04/17/How-Algorithms-and-Authoritarianism-Created-a-Corporate-Nightmare-at-United

van Rijmenam, Mark. "Algorithms Are Changing Business: Here's How to Leverage Them." *Conversation*. March 20, 2016. theconversation.com/algorithms-are-changing-business-heres-how-to-leverage-them-56281

1 | Work backward from the future

Bogost, Ian. "Apple's Airpods Are an Omen." *Atlantic*. June 12, 2018. theatlantic.com/technology/archive/2018/06/apples-airpods-are-an-omen/554537

Chandrashekar, Ashok, Fernando Amat, Justin Basilico, and Tony Jebara. "Artwork Personalization at Netflix." The Netflix Tech Blog. December 7, 2017. medium.com/netflix-techblog/artwork-personalization-c589f074ad76

Horwitz, Josh. "The Billion-Dollar, Alibaba-Backed AI Company That's Quietly Watching People in China." Quartz. April 15, 2018. qz.com/1248493/sensetime-the-billion-dollar-alibaba-backed-ai-company-thats-quietly-watching-everyone-in-china

Knight, Will. "China's AI Awakening." *MIT Technology Review*. October 10, 2017. technologyreview.com/s/609038/chinas-ai-awakening

———. "Google and Others Are Building AI Systems That Doubt Themselves." *MIT Technology Review*. January 9, 2018. technologyreview.com/s/609762/google-and-others-are-building-ai-systems-that-doubt-themselves

Madrigal, Alexis C. "Future Historians Probably Won't Understand Our Internet, and That's Okay." *Atlantic.* December 6, 2017. theatlantic.com/technology/ archive/2017/12/it-might-be-impossible-for-future-historians-to-understand-our-internet/547463

Nunes, Bernardo, and Diogo Gonçalves. "Three Ways the Internet of Things Is Shaping Consumer Behavior." Behavioral Economics. February 28, 2017. behavioraleconomics.com/three-ways-the-internet-of-things-is-shaping-consumer-behavior

Samuel, Alexandra. "Opinion: Forget 'Digital Natives.' Here's How Kids Are Really Using the Internet." TED. May 4, 2017. ideas.ted.com/opinion-forget-digital-natives-heres-how-kids-are-really-using-the-internet

Yang, Yuan, and Yingzhi Yang. "Smile to Enter: China Embraces Facial-Recognition Technology." *Financial Times.* June 7, 2017. ft.com/content/ ae2ec0ac-4744-11e7-8519-9f94ee97d996

2 | Aim for 10×, not 10%

Brynes, Nanette. "As Goldman Embraces Automation, Even the Masters of the Universe Are Threatened." *MIT Technology Review.* February 7, 2017. technologyreview.com/s/603431/as-goldman-embraces-automation-even-the-masters-of-the-universe-are-threatened

Cournoyer, J. S. "Toward an AI-First World." Real. December 14, 2017. medium.com/believing/toward-an-ai-first-world-9103374c94bc

Evans, Benedict. "The Amazon Machine." Benedict Evans. December 12, 2017. ben-evans.com/benedictevans/2017/12/12/the-amazon-machine

Gefferie, Dwayne. "Become Data-Driven or Perish: Why Your Company Needs a Data Strategy and Not Just More Data People." Towards Data Science. February 6, 2018. towardsdatascience.com/become-data-driven-or-perish-why-your-company-needs-a-data-strategy-and-not-just-more-data-people-aa5d435c2f9

Langley, Monica. "Ballmer on Ballmer: His Exit from Microsoft." *Wall Street Journal.* November 17, 2013. wsj.com/articles/ballmer-on-ballmer-his-exit-from-microsoft-1384547387

Marr, Bernard. "Really Big Data at Walmart: Real-Time Insights from Their 40+ Petabyte Data Cloud." *Forbes.* January 23, 2017. forbes.com/sites/ bernardmarr/2017/01/23/really-big-data-at-walmart-real-time-insights-from-their-40-petabyte-data-cloud/#2586a566c105

Nakashima, Ryan. "Why AI Visionary Andrew Ng Teaches Humans to Teach Computers." AP News. August 21, 2017. apnews.com/83b60f5e55f04e818 4608b0eb1bf7d0a

Rodgers, Todd, and Haven Life. "How AI Will Power the Future of Life Insurance." Venture Beat. March 30, 2017. venturebeat.com/2017/03/30/how-ai-will-power-the-future-of-life-insurance

Zeng, Ming. "Alibaba and the Future of Business." *Harvard Business Review.* October 2018. hbr.org/2018/09/alibaba-and-the-future-of-business

3 | Think computationally

Agrawal, Ajay, Joshua Gans, and Avi Goldfarb. "How AI Will Change the Way We Make Decisions." *Harvard Business Review.* July 26, 2017. hbr.org/2017/07/how-ai-will-change-the-way-we-make-decisions

Bonnington, Christina. "It Was a Big Year for A.I." Slate. December 28, 2017. slate.com/blogs/future_tense/2017/12/28/year_in_artificial_intelligence_most_impressive_ai_and_machine_learning.html

Broadbent, Andrew. "It's Not Too Late to Save Your Job from Automation." The Next Web. August 2018. thenextweb.com/contributors/2018/08/11/how-to-save-your-job-from-automation

Chen, Angela. "How AI Is Helping Us Discover Materials Faster Than Ever." The Verge. April 25, 2018. theverge.com/2018/4/25/17275270/artificial-intelligence-materials-science-computation

Chen, Sophia. "New Kepler Exoplanet Discovery Fueled by AI." *Wired.* December 14, 2017. wired.com/story/new-kepler-exoplanet-90i-discovery-fueled-by-ai

Chui, Michael, Katy George, and Mehdi Miremadi. "A CEO Action Plan for Workplace Automation." *McKinsey Quarterly.* McKinsey & Company. July 2017. mckinsey.com/featured-insights/digital-disruption/a-ceo-action-plan-for-workplace-automation

Collins, Jason. "Don't Touch the Computer." *Behavioral Scientist.* July 13, 2017. behavioralscientist.org/dont-touch-computer

———. "What to Do When Algorithms Rule." *Behavioral Scientist.* February 6, 2018. behavioralscientist.org/what-to-do-when-algorithms-rule

Dietvorst, Berkeley, Joseph P. Simmons, and Cade Massey. "Overcoming Algorithm Aversion: People Will Use Imperfect Algorithms If They Can (Even Slightly) Modify Them." April 5, 2016. ssrn.com/abstract=2616787

Gershgorn, Dave. "By Sparring with AlphaGo, Researchers Are Learning How an Algorithm Thinks." Quartz. February 16, 2017. qz.com/897498/by-sparring-with-alphago-researchers-are-learning-how-an-algorithm-thinks

Kalelioğlu, Filiz, Yasemin Gülbahar, and Volkan Kukul. "A Framework for Computational Thinking Based on a Systematic Research Review." *Baltic Journal of Modern Computing* 4 (3), 583–596. April 20, 2016. bjmc.lu.lv/fileadmin/user_upload/lu_portal/projekti/bjmc/Contents/4_3_15_Kalelioglu.pdf

Karvounis, Niko. "Three Questions to Ask Your Advanced-Analytics Team." *Harvard Business Review*. September 21, 2012. hbr.org/2012/09/three-questions-to-ask-your-ad

Li, Michael, Madina Kassengaliyeva, and Raymond Perkins. "Better Questions to Ask Your Data Scientists." *Harvard Business Review*. November 25, 2016. hbr.org/2016/11/better-questions-to-ask-your-data-scientists

McGee, Suzanne. "Rise of the Billionaire Robots: How Algorithms Have Redefined Hedge Funds." *Guardian*. May 15, 2016. theguardian.com/business/us-money-blog/2016/may/15/hedge-fund-managers-algorithms-robots-investment-tips

Miller, Claire Cain, and Jess Bidgood. "How to Prepare Preschoolers for an Automated Economy." *New York Times*. July 31, 2017. nytimes.com/2017/07/31/upshot/how-to-prepare-preschoolers-for-an-automated-economy.html

Rice, Xan. "So Much for 'The Table Never Lies': Data Unravels Football's Biggest Lie of All." *New Statesman*. February 19, 2017. newstatesman.com/politics/sport/2017/02/so-much-table-never-lies-data-unravels-footballs-biggest-lie-all

Rifkin, Glenn. "Seymour Papert, 88, Dies; Saw Education's Future in Computers." *New York Times*. August 1, 2016. nytimes.com/2016/08/02/technology/seymour-papert-88-dies-saw-educations-future-in-computers.html

Satariano, Adam, and Nishant Kumar. "The Massive Hedge Fund Betting on AI." *Bloomberg*. September 26, 2017. bloomberg.com/news/features/2017-09-27/the-massive-hedge-fund-betting-on-ai

Stokes, Jon. "How Intel Missed the iPhone Revolution." Techcrunch. May 17, 2016. techcrunch.com/2016/05/17/how-intel-missed-the-iphone-revolution

Zeng, Ming. "Alibaba and the Future of Business." *Harvard Business Review*. October 2018. hbr.org/2018/09/alibaba-and-the-future-of-business

4 | Embrace uncertainty

Blenko, Marcia W., Michael Mankins, and Paul Rogers. "The Decision-Driven Organization." *Harvard Business Review*. June 2010. hbr.org/2010/06/the-decision-driven-organization

Dörner, Karel, and Jürgen Meffert. "Nine Questions to Help You Get Your Digital Transformation Right." *McKinsey Quarterly*. McKinsey & Company. October 2015. mckinsey.com/business-functions/organization/our-insights/nine-questions-to-help-you-get-your-digital-transformation-right

Epstein, Adam. "'The Algorithm's Argument Is Gonna Win': Cary Fukunaga Explains How Data Call the Shots at Netflix." Quartz. August 28, 2018. qz.com/quartzy/1372129/maniac-director-cary-fukunaga-explains-how-data-call-the-shots-at-netflix

Fox, Justin. "From 'Economic Man' to Behavioral Economics." *Harvard Business Review*. May 2015. hbr.org/2015/05/from-economic-man-to-behavioral-economics

Gullickson, Brad. "In the Future, All Your Favorite Movies Will Be Greenlit by Artificial Intelligence." Film School Rejects. July 5, 2018. filmschoolrejects.com/in-the-future-all-your-favorite-movies-will-be-greenlit-by-artificial-intelligence

Jayadevan, P.K. "How the 'Amazon of Japan' Plans to Drink from Its Data Firehose." Factor Daily. September 18, 2017. factordaily.com/rakuten-data-strategy

Kolbert, Elizabeth. "Why Facts Don't Change Our Minds." *New Yorker*. February 27, 2017. newyorker.com/magazine/2017/02/27/why-facts-dont-change-our-minds

Li, Michael, Madina Kassengaliyeva, and Raymond Perkins. "Better Questions to Ask Your Data Scientists." *Harvard Business Review*. November 25, 2016. hbr.org/2016/11/better-questions-to-ask-your-data-scientists

Pettingill, Lindsay M. "4 Principles for Making Experimentation Count." Airbnb Engineering & Data Science Blog. March 21, 2017. medium.com/airbnb-engineering/4-principles-for-making-experimentation-count-7a5f1a5268a

Rana, Zat. "Jeff Bezos: How to Make Smart Decisions." Personal Growth. September 21, 2017. medium.com/personal-growth/what-you-can-learn-from-jeff-bezos-and-amazon-about-achieving-your-goals-30701ef1f3c

Schrage, Michael. "4 Models for Using AI to Make Decisions." *Harvard Business Review*. January 27, 2017. hbr.org/2017/01/4-models-for-using-ai-to-make-decisions

Tampio, Nicholas. "Look up from Your Screen." Aeon. August 2, 2018. aeon.co/essays/children-learn-best-when-engaged-in-the-living-world-not-on-screens

Thau, Barbara. "J.C. Penney and Macy's Replace Human Merchants with Data Algorithms." *Forbes*. November 6, 2017. forbes.com/sites/barbarathau/2017/11/06/j-c-penney-and-macys-replace-human-merchants-with-data-algorithms/#62338b986c17

5 | Make culture your operating system

Alsever, Jennifer. "Is Software Better at Managing People Than You Are?" *Fortune*. March 21, 2016. fortune.com/2016/03/21/software-algorithms-hiring

Bliss, Laura. "How WeWork Has Perfectly Captured the Millennial Id." *Atlantic*. March 2018. theatlantic.com/magazine/archive/2018/03/wework-the-perfect-manifestation-of-the-millennial-id/550922

Kessler, Sarah. "IBM, Remote-Work Pioneer, Is Calling Thousands of Employees Back to the Office." Quartz. March 21, 2017. qz.com/924167/ibm-remote-work-pioneer-is-calling-thousands-of-employees-back-to-the-office

Kostov, Nick, and David Gauthier-Villars. "Advertising's 'Mad Men' Bristle at the Digital Revolution." *Wall Street Journal.* January 19, 2018. wsj.com/articles/ data-revolution-upends-madison-avenue-1516383643

Nadella, Satya. "Microsoft's Next Act." *McKinsey Quarterly.* McKinsey & Company. April 2018. mckinsey.com/industries/high-tech/our-insights/ microsofts-next-act

Schneider, Michael. "Google Spent 2 Years Studying 180 Teams. The Most Successful Ones Shared These 5 Traits." Inc. inc.com/michael-schneider/ google-thought-they-knew-how-to-create-the-perfect.html

Strauss, Valerie. "The Surprising Thing Google Learned about Its Employees— and What It Means for Today's Students." *Washington Post.* December 20, 2017. washingtonpost.com/news/answer-sheet/wp/2017/12/20/the- surprising-thing-google-learned-about-its-employees-and-what-it-means-for- todays-students

6 | Don't work, design work

Bessen, James. "How Computer Automation Affects Occupations: Technology, Jobs, and Skills." Vox. September 22, 2016. voxeu.org/article/how-computer- automation-affects-occupations

Cohen, Steven, A. Granade, and W. Matthew. "Models Will Run the World." *Wall Street Journal.* August 19, 2018. wsj.com/articles/models-will-run- the-world-1534716720

Cresci, Elena. "Chatbot that Overturned 160,000 Parking Fines Now Helping Refugees Claim Asylum." *Guardian.* March 6, 2017. theguardian.com/ technology/2017/mar/06/chatbot-donotpay-refugees-claim-asylum-legal-aid

Davenport, Tom. "The Rise of Cognitive Work (Re)Design: Applying Cognitive Tools to Knowledge-Based Work." Deloitte. July 31, 2017. www2.deloitte .com/insights/us/en/deloitte-review/issue-21/applying-cognitive-tools-to- knowledge-work.html

Dormehl, Luke. "Meet the British Whiz Kid Who Fights for Justice with a Robo-Lawyer Sidekick." Digital Trends. March 25, 2018. digitaltrends.com/ cool-tech/robot-lawyer-free-acess-justice

Kamer, Jurriaan. "How to Build Your Own Spotify Model." The Ready. February 9, 2018. medium.com/the-ready/how-to-build-your-own-spotify-model- dce98025d32f

Knight, Will. "The Machines Are Getting Ready to Play Doctor." *MIT Technology Review.* July 7, 2017. technologyreview.com/s/608234/the-machines-are- getting-ready-to-play-doctor

Wang, Dan. "How Technology Grows (A Restatement of Definite Optimism)." Dan Wang. July 24, 2018. danwang.co/how-technology-grows

7 | Automate and elevate

Autor, David H. "Skills, Education, and the Rise of Earnings Inequality among the Other 99 Percent." *Science* 344 (6186), 843–851. May 23, 2014. science.sciencemag.org/content/344/6186/843

Baraniuk, Chris. "How Algorithms Run Amazon's Warehouses." BBC. August 18, 2015. bbc.com/future/story/20150818-how-algorithms-run-amazons-warehouses

Bessen, James. "How Computer Automation Affects Occupations: Technology, Jobs, and Skills." Vox. September 22, 2016. voxeu.org/article/how-computer-automation-affects-occupations

Byrnes, Nanette. "As Goldman Embraces Automation, Even the Masters of the Universe Are Threatened." *MIT Technology Review*. February 7, 2017. technologyreview.com/s/603431/as-goldman-embraces-automation-even-the-masters-of-the-universe-are-threatened

Dewhurst, Martin, and Paul Willmott. "Manager and Machine: The New Leadership Equation." *McKinsey Quarterly*. McKinsey & Company. September 2014. mckinsey.com/featured-insights/leadership/manager-and-machine

Dixon, Lauren. "7 Steps to Rethink Jobs in the Age of Automation." Talent Economy. February 22, 2017. clomedia.com/2017/02/22/7-steps-rethink-jobs-age-automation

Donovan, John, and Cathy Benko. "AT&T's Talent Overhaul." *Harvard Business Review*. October 2016. hbr.org/2016/10/atts-talent-overhaul

Goodman, Peter S. "The Robots Are Coming, and Sweden Is Fine." *New York Times*. December 27, 2017. nytimes.com/2017/12/27/business/the-robots-are-coming-and-sweden-is-fine.html

Khalid, Asma. "From Post-it Notes to Algorithms: How Automation Is Changing Legal Work." *All Things Considered*. National Public Radio. November 7, 2017. npr.org/sections/alltechconsidered/2017/11/07/561631927/from-post-it-notes-to-algorithms-how-automation-is-changing-legal-work

Kolbjørnsrud, Vegard, Richard Amico, and Robert J. Thomas. "How Artificial Intelligence Will Redefine Management." *Harvard Business Review*. November 2, 2016. hbr.org/2016/11/how-artificial-intelligence-will-redefine-management

Kumar, Ritwik, Vinith Misra, Jen Walraven, Lavanya Sharan, Bahareh Azarnoush, Boris Chen, and Nirmal Govind. "Data Science and the Art of Producing Entertainment at Netflix." The Netflix Tech Blog. March 26, 2018. medium.com/netflix-techblog/studio-production-data-science-646ee2cc21a1

Larson, Christina. "Closing the Factory Doors." *Foreign Policy*. July 16, 2018. foreignpolicy.com/2018/07/16/closing-the-factory-doors-manufacturing-economy-automation-jobs-developing

Lee, Thomas. "New Technology Means New Opportunities—and Anxiety for Today's Workers." *San Francisco Chronicle*. October 17, 2017. sfchronicle.com/business/article/New-technology-means-new-opportunities-and-12282975.php

Manyika, James, and Michael Spence. "The False Choice between Automation and Jobs." *Harvard Business Review*. February 5, 2018. hbr.org/2018/02/the-false-choice-between-automation-and-jobs

Martinho-Truswell, Antone. "To Automate Is Human." Aeon. February 13, 2018. aeon.co/essays/the-offloading-ape-the-human-is-the-beast-that-automates

Metz, Cade. "I Took the AI Class Facebookers Are Literally Sprinting to Get Into." *Wired*. March 27, 2017. wired.com/2017/03/took-ai-class-facebookers-literally-sprinting-get

Mims, Christopher. "Automation Can Actually Create More Jobs." *Wall Street Journal*. December 11, 2016. wsj.com/articles/automation-can-actually-create-more-jobs-1481480200

Miranda, Carolina A. "The Unbearable Awkwardness of Automation." *Atlantic*. June 13, 2018. theatlantic.com/technology/archive/2018/06/the-unbearable-awkwardness-of-automation/562670

Pichai, Sundar. "Digital Technology Must Empower Workers, Not Alienate Them." Recode. January 18, 2018. recode.net/2018/1/18/16906970/sundar-pichai-google-alphabet-skills-employment-jobs-education-code-coding-workers

Pistrui, Joseph. "The Future of Human Work Is Imagination, Creativity, and Strategy." *Harvard Business Review*. January 18, 2018. hbr.org/2018/01/the-future-of-human-work-is-imagination-creativity-and-strategy

Pitney, Nico. "Inside the Mind That Built Google Brain: On Life, Creativity, and Failure." *Huffington Post*. December 6, 2017 (updated). huffingtonpost.com/2015/05/13/andrew-ng_n_7267682.html

Pressman, Aaron. "Can AT&T Retrain 100,000 People?" *Fortune*. March 15, 2017. fortune.com/att-hr-retrain-employees-jobs-best-companies

Remus, Dana, and Frank S. Levy. "Can Robots Be Lawyers? Computers, Lawyers, and the Practice of Law." November 27, 2016. https://papers.ssrn.com/sol3/papers.cfm?abstract_id=2701092

Shestakofsky, Ben. "High-Tech Hand Work: When Humans Replace Computers, What Does It Mean for Jobs and for Technological Change?" The Castac Blog. July 7, 2015. blog.castac.org/2015/07/high-tech-handwork

Smith, Noah. "As Long as There Are Humans, There Will Be Jobs." *Bloomberg*. March 23, 2018. bloomberg.com/view/articles/2018-03-23/robots-won-t-take-all-jobs-because-humans-demand-new-things

Woyke, Elizabeth. "AI Can Now Tell Your Boss What Skills You Lack—and How You Can Get Them." *MIT Technology Review*. August 7, 2018. technologyreview.com/s/611790/coursera-ai-skills

8 | If the answer Is X, ask Y

Angwin, Julia, Jeff Larson, Surya Mattu, and Lauren Kirchner. "Machine Bias."
ProPublica. May 23, 2016. propublica.org/article/machine-bias-risk-
assessments-in-criminal-sentencing

Baer, Tobias, and Vishnu Kamalnath. "Controlling Machine-Learning
Algorithms and Their Biases." *McKinsey Quarterly*. McKinsey & Company.
November 2017. mckinsey.com/business-functions/risk/our-insights/
controlling-machine-learning-algorithms-and-their-biases

Barnes, Eric. "'Deep Patient' May Point the Way to Better Care." Auntminnie.
May 11, 2017. auntminnie.com/index.aspx?sec=seR&Sub=deF&Pag=
diS&ItemID=117351

Barocas, Solon, Sophie Hood, and Malte Ziewitz. "Governing Algorithms:
A Provocation Piece." Governing Algorithms. March 29, 2013.
governingalgorithms.org/resources/provocation-piece

Booth, Adrian, Niko Mohr, and Peter Peters. "The Digital Utility: New
Opportunities and Challenges." *McKinsey Quarterly*. McKinsey & Company.
May 2016. mckinsey.com/industries/electric-power-and-natural-gas/
our-insights/the-digital-utility-new-opportunities-and-challenges

Brauneis, Robert, and Ellen P. Goodman. "Algorithmic Transparency for the
Smart City." August 2, 2017. *Yale Journal of Law & Technology* 103 (2018);
GWU Law School Public Law Research Paper. ssrn.com/abstract=3012499

De Langhe, Bart, Stefano Puntoni, and Richard Larrick. "Linear Thinking in a
Nonlinear World." *Harvard Business Review*. June 2018. hbr.org/2017/05/
linear-thinking-in-a-nonlinear-world

Denyer, Simon. "In China, Facial Recognition Is Sharp End of a Drive for Total
Surveillance." *Chicago Tribune*. January 7, 2018. chicagotribune.com/news/
nationworld/ct-china-facial-recognition-surveillance-20180107-story.html

Dilger, Daniel Eran. "Editorial: More Companies Need to Temper Their
Artificial Intelligence with Authentic Ethics." Apple Insider. May 25, 2018.
appleinsider.com/articles/18/05/25/editorial-more-companies-need-to-
temper-their-artificial-intelligence-with-authentic-ethics

Dykes, Brent. "Crawl with Analytics before Running with Artificial Intelligence."
Forbes. January 11, 2017. forbes.com/sites/brentdykes/2017/01/11/crawl-with-
analytics-before-running-with-artificial-intelligence/#2cbf86dc299c

Knight, Will. "The Dark Secret at the Heart of AI." *MIT Technology Review*.
April 11, 2017. technologyreview.com/s/604087/the-dark-secret-at-the-
heart-of-ai

——. "The Financial World Wants to Open AI's Black Boxes." *MIT Technology
Review*. April 13, 2017. technologyreview.com/s/604122/the-financial-
world-wants-to-open-ais-black-boxes

————. "The U.S. Military Wants Its Autonomous Machines to Explain Themselves." *MIT Technology Review*. March 14, 2017. technologyreview.com/ s/603795/the-us-military-wants-its-autonomous-machines-to-explain- themselves

Kosinski, Michal, David Stillwell, and Thore Graepel. "Private Traits and Attributes Are Predictable from Digital Records of Human Behavior." PNAS. April 9, 2013. pnas.org/content/110/15/5802

Kuchler, Hannah. "Facebook Official's Memo Urged Staff to Collect Less Data." *Financial Times*. July 24, 2018. ft.com/content/9850b9ba-8f92-11e8-b639- 7680cedcc421

Peters, Adele. "This Tool Lets You See—and Correct—the Bias in an Algorithm." *Fast Company*. June 12, 2018. fastcompany.com/40583554/this-tool-lets-you- see-and-correct-the-bias-in-an-algorithm

Pinchai, Sundar. "AI at Google: Our Principles." The Keyword Blog. June 7, 2018. blog.google/technology/ai/ai-principles

Prudente, Tim. "Baltimore Mayor to Bring in Crime Fighting Strategist with High-Tech Policing Model." *Baltimore Sun*. January 31, 2018. baltimoresun .com/news/maryland/crime/bs-md-ci-sean-malinowski-20180123-story.html

Rosane, Olivia. "Beyond Machine Sight: What We Miss When We Privilege the Eye in Digital Discourse." *Real Life*. December 14, 2017. reallifemag.com/ beyond-machine-sight

Ruddick, Graham. "Facebook Forces Admiral to Pull Plan to Price Car Insurance Based on Posts." *Guardian*. November 2, 2016. theguardian.com/money/ 2016/nov/02/facebook-admiral-car-insurance-privacy-data

Thornhill, John. "Only Human Intelligence Can Solve the AI Challenge." *Financial Times*. April 17, 2017. ft.com/content/ad1b7e86-2349-11e7-a34a- 538b4cb30025

Voosen, Paul. "How AI Detectives Are Cracking Open the Black Box of Deep Learning." *Science*. July 6, 2017. sciencemag.org/news/2017/07/how-ai- detectives-are-cracking-open-black-box-deep-learning

Weinberger, David. "Optimization over Explanation." Berkman Klein Center. January 28, 2018. medium.com/berkman-klein-center/optimization- over-explanation-41ecb135763d

9 | When in doubt, ask a human

Bergstein, Brian. "The Great AI Paradox." *MIT Technology Review*. December 15, 2017. technologyreview.com/s/609318/the-great-ai-paradox

Courage, Catherine. "A Year of Learning and Leading UX at Google." Google Design. January 11, 2017. medium.com/google-design/a-year-of-learning-and- leading-ux-at-google-c81577b3cb56

Dotson, Kyt. "AI-Augmented Crowdsourcing Company Crowdflower Raises $20M for Enterprise Push." Silicon Angle. June 15, 2017. siliconangle .com/2017/06/12/ai-augmented-crowdsourced-labor-company-crowdflower-raises-20m-funding

Girling, Rob. "AI and the Future of Design: What Will the Designer of 2025 Look Like?" O'Reilly. January 4, 2017. oreilly.com/ideas/ai-and-the-future-of-design-what-will-the-designer-of-2025-look-like

Golden, Paul. "Asset Managers Turn to Machine Leading." Global Investor. June 9, 2017. globalinvestorgroup.com/articles/3687955/asset-managers-turn-to-machine-leading

Guszcza, Jim. "Smarter Together: Why Artificial Intelligence Needs Human-Centered Design." Deloitte Insights. *Deloitte Review* 22. January 22, 2018. www2.deloitte.com/insights/us/en/deloitte-review/issue-22/artificial-intelligence-human-centric-design.html

Harvey, Hugh. "Why AI Will Not Replace Radiologists." Towards Data Science. January 24, 2018. towardsdatascience.com/why-ai-will-not-replace-radiologists-c7736f2c7d80

Ito, Joi. "AI Engineers Must Open Their Designs to Democratic Control." ACLU. April 2, 2018. aclu.org/issues/privacy-technology/surveillance-technologies/ai-engineers-must-open-their-designs-democratic?redirect=issues/privacy-technology/consumer-privacy/ai-engineers-must-open-their-designs-democratic-control

Jana, Reena. "Exploring and Visualizing an Open Global Dataset." Google AI Blog. August 25, 2017. ai.googleblog.com/2017/08/exploring-and-visualizing-open-global.html

Kumar, Nishant. "How AI Will Invade Every Corner of Wall Street." *Bloomberg*. December 4, 2017. bloomberg.com/news/features/2017-12-05/how-ai-will-invade-every-corner-of-wall-street

Lovejoy, Josh, and Jess Holbrook. "Human-Centered Machine Learning." Google Design. July 9, 2017. medium.com/google-design/human-centered-machine-learning-a770d10562cd

Sinders, Caroline. "The Most Crucial Design Job of the Future." *Fast Company*. July 24, 2017. fastcompany.com/90134155/the-most-crucial-design-job-of-the-future

Takahashi, Lico. "AI and Human-Centered Design: What's the Future?" UX Collective. October 28, 2017. uxdesign.cc/ai-and-human-centered-design-whats-the-future-5c88f523c07a

Wojcicki, Susan. "Expanding Our Work against Abuse of Our Platform." YouTube Official Blog. December 4, 2017. youtube.googleblog.com/2017/12/expanding-our-work-against-abuse-of-our.html

10 | Solve for purpose, not just profit

Goldhill, Olivia. "Time Is a Human Invention That Controls How We Work." *Quartz.* January 28, 2018. qz.com/1188370/time-is-a-human-invention-that-controls-how-we-work

Goler, Lori, Janelle Gale, Brynn Harrington, and Adam Grant. "Why People Really Quit Their Jobs." *Harvard Business Review.* January 11, 2018. hbr.org/2018/01/why-people-really-quit-their-jobs

Harter, Jim. "Dismal Employee Engagement Is a Sign of Global Mismanagement." Gallup Blog. December 20, 2017. news.gallup.com/opinion/gallup/224012/dismal-employee-engagement-sign-global-mismanagement.aspx

Hodgson, Camilla. "IBM looks for caffeine buzz with coffee delivery drones." *Financial Times.* August 22, 2018. ft.com/content/51a801b2-a464-11e8-8ecf-a7ae1beff35b

Manyika, James, and Matthew Taylor. "How Do We Create Meaningful Work in an Age of Automation?" *McKinsey Quarterly.* McKinsey & Company. February 2018. mckinsey.com/featured-insights/future-of-work/how-do-we-create-meaningful-work-in-an-age-of-automation

Merrick, Amy. "Walmart's Future Workforce: Robots and Freelancers." *Atlantic.* April 4, 2018. theatlantic.com/business/archive/2018/04/walmarts-future-workforce-robots-and-freelancers/557063

Newport, Cal. "Beyond Black Box Management." Cal Newport Blog. April 21, 2018. calnewport.com/blog/2018/04/21/beyond-black-box-management

O'Connor, Sarah. "When Your Boss Is an Algorithm." *Financial Times.* September 7, 2016. ft.com/content/88fdc58e-754f-11e6-b60a-de4532d5ea35

Rothschild, Viola. "China's Gig Economy Is Driving Close to the Edge." Foreign Policy. September 7, 2018. foreignpolicy.com/2018/09/07/chinas-gig-economy-is-driving-close-to-the-edge

Sapone, Marcela. "Job Titles Make Everyone Worse at Their Jobs." *Quartz.* February 1, 2018. qz.com/work/1195640/job-titles-are-making-everyone-worse-at-their-jobs

Solon, Olivia. "The Rise of 'Pseudo-AI': How Tech Firms Quietly Use Humans to Do Bots' Work." *Guardian.* July 6, 2018. theguardian.com/technology/2018/jul/06/artificial-intelligence-ai-humans-bots-tech-companies

Weber, Lauren. "Some of the World's Largest Employers No Longer Sell Things, They Rent Workers." *Wall Street Journal.* December 28, 2017. wsj.com/articles/some-of-the-worlds-largest-employers-no-longer-sell-things-they-rent-workers-1514479580

Wolcott, Robert C. "How Automation Will Change Work, Purpose, and Meaning." *Harvard Business Review.* January 11, 2018. hbr.org/2018/01/how-automation-will-change-work-purpose-and-meaning

ABOUT THE AUTHOR

Mike Walsh is the CEO of Tomorrow, a global consultancy on designing companies for the twenty-first century. He advises leaders on how to thrive in the current era of disruptive technological change.

A true global nomad, Mike travels over 300 days a year worldwide, researching trends, collecting case studies, and presenting on the future of business. Mike's clients include many of the global Fortune 500, and as a sought-after keynote speaker he regularly shares the stage with world leaders and business icons alike. Mike previously founded Jupiter Research in Australia, and has also held senior strategy roles at News Corporation in the Asia Pacific region.

Mike's other books include *Futuretainment* and *The Dictionary of Dangerous Ideas*. Each week he interviews provocative thinkers, innovators, and troublemakers on his podcast, *Between Worlds*.

www.mike-walsh.com

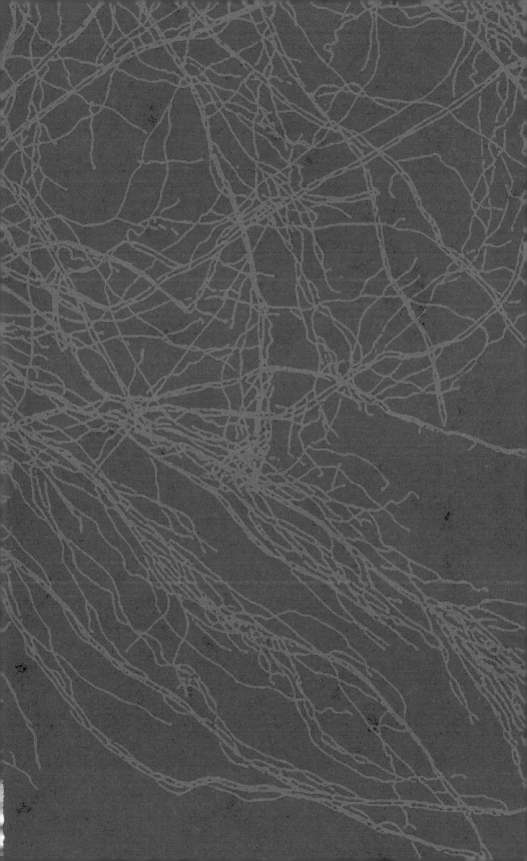

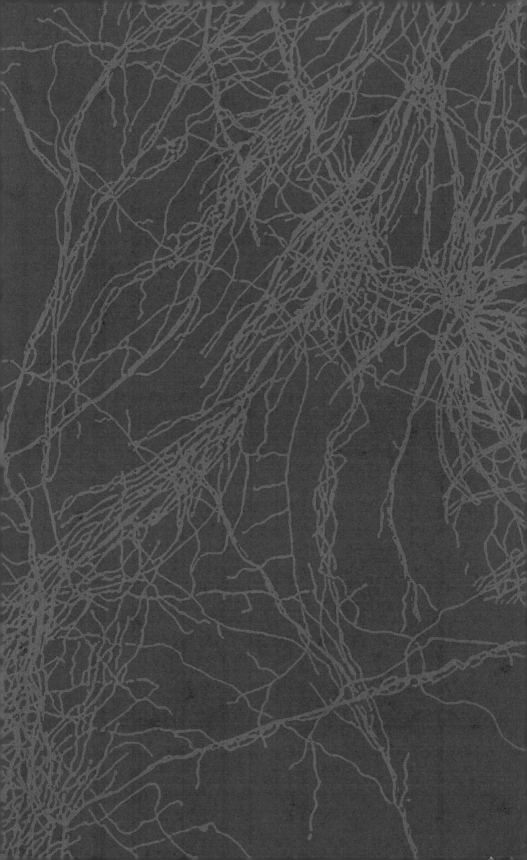